# The Novels of
# John le Carré

## The Art of
## Survival

DAVID MONAGHAN

Basil Blackwell

© David Monaghan 1985

First published 1985

Basil Blackwell Ltd
108 Cowley Road, Oxford OX4 1JF, UK

Basil Blackwell Inc.
432 Park Avenue South, Suite 1505,
New York, NY 10016, USA

**British Library Cataloguing in Publication Data**

Monaghan, David
    The novels of John le Carré.
    1. Le Carré, John———Criticism and
interpretation
    I. Title
    823'.914     PR6053.074Z/
    ISBN 0-631-14283-5

**Library of Congress Cataloging in Publication Data**

Monaghan, David.
    The novels of John le Carré.
    Bibliography: p.
    Includes index.
    1. Le Carré, John, 1931–    ———Criticism and
interpretation. 2 Spy stories, English———History and
criticism.  I. Title.
    PR6062.E33Z78  1985     823'.914     85-4058
    ISBN 0-631-14283-5

Typeset by Freeman Graphic, Tonbridge, Kent
Printed in Great Britain by Billings Ltd, Worcester

# Contents

# Acknowledgements

I am particularly grateful to John le Carré for his kindness in granting permission to quote from his novels. However, John le Carré has not read the text of this work and his permission does not therefore constitute an approval of its general contents or of my critical opinions. Others to whom I owe a debt include the Humanities and Social Sciences Research Council of Canada for the award of a Leave Fellowship in 1983–4, during which time most of this book was written; Mount Saint Vincent University for research grants; the staff of the British Library, the Bodleian Library, the BBC Script Library and Mount Saint Vincent University Library; Judith A. Kavanagh for editing and typing; George Greenfield of John Farquharson for his help in obtaining permissions; the colleagues and friends who brought to my attention new material on le Carré.

# Abbreviations and le Carré Editions

CD    *Call for the Dead* (1961) from *The le Carré Omnibus* (London: Gollancz, 1969)

MQ    *A Murder of Quality* (1962) from *The le Carré Omnibus* (London: Gollancz, 1969)

SC    *The Spy Who Came in from the Cold* (1963) (London: Gollancz, 1964)

LG    *The Looking-Glass War* (London: Heinemann, 1965)

ST    *A Small Town in Germany* (London: Heinemann, 1968)

NS    *The Naive and Sentimental Lover* (London: Hodder and Stoughton, 1971)

TT    *Tinker, Tailor, Soldier, Spy* (London: Hodder and Stoughton, 1974)

HS    *The Honourable Schoolboy* (London: Hodder and Stoughton, 1977)

SP    *Smiley's People* (London: Hodder and Stoughton, 1980)

LD    *The Little Drummer Girl* (London: Hodder and Stoughton, 1983)

All references in the text are to the editions cited above. Other first British editions of le Carré's novels are as follows:

*Call for the Dead* (London: Gollancz, 1961)
*A Murder of Quality* (London: Gollancz, 1962)

*The Quest for Karla* (omnibus edition of *Tinker, Tailor, Soldier, Spy, The Honourable Schoolboy* and *Smiley's People,* London: Hodder and Stoughton, 1982)

First American editions of le Carré's novels are as follows:

*Call for the Dead* (New York: Walker and Co., 1962)
*A Murder of Quality* (New York: Walker and Co., 1963)
*The Incongruous Spy* (omnibus edition of *Call for the Dead* and *A Murder of Quality* New York: Walker and Co., 1964)
*The Spy Who Came in from the Cold* (New York: Coward-McCann, 1964)
*The Looking Glass War* (New York: Coward-McCann, 1965)
*A Small Town in Germany* (New York: Coward-McCann, 1968)
*The Naive and Sentimental Lover* (New York: Knopf, 1972)
*Tinker, Tailor, Soldier, Spy* (New York: Knopf, 1974)
*The Honourable Schoolboy* (New York: Knopf, 1977)
*Smiley's People* (New York: Knopf, 1980)
*The Quest for Karla* (New York: Knopf, 1982)
*The Little Drummer Girl* (New York: Knopf, 1983)

Le Carré's novels are published in paperback in Britain by Pan except for *Call for the Dead* and *A Murder of Quality* which are published by Penguin. In the USA Bantam has published all le Carré's novels in paperback.

# Introduction

JOHN LE CARRÉ has taught his whippets, Mach II and
Whisper, to growl on hearing the word 'critic'.[1] In a
broad sense his hostility is quite understandable, for many
creative artists take offence at an activity which they
consider parasitic; the jazz cornet player Muggsy Spanier
even goes so far as to dedicate his composition 'Feather
Brain Blues' to the critics.[2] However, le Carré has little real
cause to complain at the specific way in which critics have
handled his work. This is not to say that all of them have
been kind or even just. *The Naive and Sentimental Lover*
was generally savaged and at various times le Carré has
been described as sentimental, long-winded or pretentious,
and his novels dismissed as guide books or documentaries
which lack atmosphere or adequate characterization.[3] But

[1] Mark Abley, 'John le Carré's Trail of Terror', *Maclean's*, 7 March 1983,
p. 52.
[2] See Albert McCarthy's sleeve notes for the record *Muggsy Spanier* released by
Storyville Records in 1968. 'Feather Brain Blues' is the third track on side two of
this record.
[3] A typical review of *The Naive and Sentimental Lover*, which describes the
novel as 'a disastrous failure', is 'Wishful Thinking', *Times Literary Supplement*,
24 Sept. 1971, p. 1138. Others who have not been impressed with le Carré's
work include Anthony Burgess, 'Peking Drugs, Moscow Gold', rev. of *The
Honourable Schoolboy*, *New York Times Book Review*, 25 Sept. 1977, pp. 9,
45; David Caute, 'It Was a Man', rev. of *Smiley's People*, *New Statesman*, 8 Feb.
1980, p. 209; Louis Finger, 'The Manly One', rev. of *The Honourable Schoolboy*, *New Statesman*, 23 Sept. 1977, pp. 414–15; Clive James, 'Go Back to the
Cold!', rev. of *The Honourable Schoolboy*, *New York Review of Books*, 27 Oct.
1977, pp. 29–30; L. R. Leavis and J. M. Blom, 'Current Literature, 1977', rev. of

what is more significant is that those critics who have
written sympathetically about his work have been refresh-
ingly free from the kind of prejudice against genre fiction
which, in the past, has prevented a proper evaluation of
the worth of a number of significant novelists, most
notably Dashiell Hammett and Raymond Chandler. As a
result they have been willing to judge le Carré in relation to
the best of his contemporaries and to define his achievement in literary terms.

Among those who make large claims for le Carré are
George Grella who asserts that he is 'one of the best living
English writers'[4] and T. G. Rosenthal for whom he is 'not
really a thriller writer at all, but one of the best novelists
we have'.[5] Le Carré's importance has been variously ex-
plained. William F. Buckley jr is impressed by the subtlety
of his analysis of contemporary society[6] while Anatole
Broyard points to the profundity of his broader themes
which are focused on a conflict between the 'unruly'
human heart and dehumanizing bureaucracy.[7] Others
emphasize his achievements in technique. V. S. Pritchett,
for example, points to George Smiley's complexity as a
character,[8] Tom Paulin to the mythopoeic aspects of
le Carré's work and to his symbolically charged land-

---

The Honourable Schoolboy, English Studies, 59 (1978), p. 447; Derek Mahon,
'Dolls within Dolls', rev. of Tinker, Tailor, Soldier, Spy, Listener, 92 (4 July
1974), p. 30; Lord Vaizey, 'Futile Jerry', rev. of The Honourable Schoolboy,
Listener, 98 (29 Sept. 1977), p. 409.

[4] 'John le Carré: Murder and Loyalty, New Republic, 175 (31 July 1976), p. 24.

[5] 'Thrillers into Novels', rev. of A Small Town in Germany, New Statesman, 8
Nov. 1968, p. 641.

[6] 'Terror and a Woman', rev. of The Little Drummer Girl, New York Times
Book Review, 13 March 1983, p. 23.

[7] 'Le Carré's People', rev. of The Quest for Karla, New York Times Book
Review, 29 Aug. 1982, p. 23.

[8] 'A Spy Romance', rev. of Smiley's People, New York Review of Books, 7 Feb.
1980, p. 22.

scapes,[9] James Wolcott to his unifying metaphors,[10] and T. J. Binyon to his flexible narrative voice.[11]

Several critics have also established that le Carré's use of popular conventions, far from being irrelevant or even detrimental, has a central role to play in his achievement. T. J. Binyon, for example, argues that part of what makes *The Honourable Schoolboy* into 'a substantial novel' is its ironic assimilation of 'the former tradition' of the spy novel,[12] and Al Alvarez that, in *Smiley's People,* le Carré has 'once again turned the novel of action into a novel of character and motivation'.[13] Le Carré's further use of spying as a metaphor for modern society is a topic touched on by both George Grella[14] and Andrew Rutherford.[15]

There is, then, a well-established body of opinion to support the notion that le Carré is a significant writer worthy of critical analysis. Up to this time, however, almost everything which is illuminating about him is also brief. With the notable exception of Andrew Rutherford's excellent chapter on le Carré's relationship to the traditional spy novel,[16] more extended studies of his work, such as Gillespie's analysis of the spy as alien,[17] Rothberg's examination of George Smiley's development,[18] Halperin's

[9] 'National Myths: Recent Fiction', rev. of *Smiley's People, Encounter,* 54 (June 1980), pp. 58–60.
[10] 'The Secret Sharers', rev. of *The Little Drummer Girl, New York Review of Books,* 14 April 1983, pp. 19–21.
[11] 'A Gentleman Among Players', rev. of *The Honourable Schoolboy, Times Literary Supplement,* 9 Sept. 1977, p. 1069.
[12] Ibid.
[13] 'Half-Angels Versus Half-Devils', rev. of *Smiley's People, Observer,* 3 Feb. 1980, p. 39.
[14] 'John le Carré: Murder and Loyalty', pp. 23–5.
[15] 'The Spy as Hero: le Carré and the Cold War', in *The Literature of War. Five Studies of Heroic Virtue* (London: Macmillan, 1978), p. 150.
[16] Ibid., pp. 135–56.
[17] Robert Gillespie, 'Secret Agents and the Cold War', *Salmagundi,* 13 (Summer 1970), pp. 45–60.
[18] Abraham Rothberg, 'The Decline and Fall of George Smiley: John le Carré and English Decency', *Southwest Review,* 66 (Autumn 1981), pp. 377–93.

attempt to define le Carré's central concerns and authentic sources,[19] and Panek's study of his place in the history of the spy novel,[20] have been either unoriginal or misleading. Consequently, the present work has no large foundations upon which to build. Nevertheless, those small foundations which do exist are solid and I take as my basic assumption that le Carré's readers are ready for something more challenging and substantial than a mere introduction to his works. Thus, no plot summaries or character sketches are provided here. Nor is there any outline of the author's life, for this is readily available elsewhere.[21] Instead my book consists of five closely related essays which seek to identify and to elucidate what I, and some of the critics discussed above, consider to be those aspects of le Carré's art which are central to an understanding of his major concerns and achievement.

Chapter 1 takes as its subject le Carré's dualistic vision of experience. For le Carré, every individual personality is divided between the contradictory claims of reflection and feeling, or what Schiller calls the naive and the sentimental. The reconciliation of these divergent forces must be the goal of anyone who would achieve complete maturity. And yet, as Schiller and le Carré point out, such a reconciliation is impossible. This is especially true in a society such as contemporary Britain which places little value on

[19] John Halperin, 'Between Two Worlds: The Novels of John le Carré', *South Atlantic Quarterly*, 79 (Winter 1980), pp. 17–37.
[20] Leroy L. Panek, 'John le Carré' in *The Special Branch: The British Spy Novel, 1890–1980* (Bowling Green: Bowling Green Univ. Popular Press, 1981), pp. 236–57.
[21] See for example, Abley, 'John le Carré's Trail of Terror', pp. 47–52; Arnold W. Ehrlich, '*PW* Interviews: John le Carré', *Publisher's Weekly*, 212, 19 Sept. 1977, pp. 56–8; Miriam Gross, 'The Secret World of John le Carré', *Observer*, 3 Feb. 1980, pp. 33–5; John le Carré, 'England Made Me', *Observer*, 13 Nov. 1977, p. 25. For information about le Carré's supposed involvement in espionage, see Alexis Gelber and Edward Behr, 'The Spymaster Returns', *Newsweek*, 7 March 1983, pp. 70–1.

feeling, spontaneity or individuality. As a result, so le Carré claims, most people eschew the search for self and take refuge in cultivating one pole of experience at the expense of the other. Thus, much of his fictional energy is devoted to charting the various strategies adopted by his characters to produce these polarised solutions to the essentially complex problems of living. The satirical emphasis which this creates is reinforced by the failure of almost every character who takes on the challenge of integrating the divergent claims of feeling and reflection. Le Carré's novels are saved from complete pessimism, however, by the presence, at the centre of a number of them, of that product of the author's self-professed romanticism, George Smiley, a man who never flinches from the task of becoming a full and complex human being.

The methods which le Carré employs to give expression to his central thematic preoccupation are the subject of the next three chapters. Chapter 2 concerns itself with le Carré's creation of the symbolic landscapes which carry the main burden of his analysis of modern society. It demonstrates that Western and Eastern Europe and the USA are in much the same spiritual condition as Britain, and that nowhere except in Chinese Hong Kong does an environment exist in which the individual's impulse towards complete humanity receives any nourishment. Le Carré's world is, symbolically speaking, a dark place and only Hong Kong possesses any light. However, the extension of the pattern of dark–light imagery into the realm of individual behaviour enables le Carré to offer the romantic conclusion that each of us possesses the ability to restore at least some illumination to the dark landscape.

The need to find metaphors capable of expressing the tension between a cynical social analysis and romantic affirmation also provides the key to an understanding of le Carré's relationship to the spy novel tradition, which is the topic of chapter 3. His most obvious allegiance is to the 'realistic' spy novels of Joseph Conrad and Graham Greene which provide valuable models of how the subject of espionage can be made to serve as a vehicle for social satire. However, this chapter argues that le Carré is equally indebted to the popular spy novel for providing a myth of the ideal society in which a proper balance is achieved between the needs of individual and group.

Important as le Carré's use of light imagery and of the popular spy novel are in providing a counterbalance to the cynicism and pessimism which pervade his novels, the main burden of affirmation falls nevertheless on his central seeker after humanity, George Smiley. Thus, any change in outlook that Smiley might experience in the course of his fictional career will have important implications for the tone and emphasis of le Carré's novels. Chapter 4, which deals with Smiley's recurring role, argues that, contrary to the claims of some critics and even of the author, Smiley retains essentially the same approach to experience in every novel in which he appears, and thus continues to be a vehicle for the expression of le Carré's faith in the persistence of the human urge towards completeness. The second part of the chapter demonstrates that, far from seeking to change Smiley, le Carré has been endeavouring throughout his career to develop ever more sophisticated ways of expressing his initial conception of the character.

The unity of le Carré's fiction is also the topic of the final chapter which is concerned with the implications of le Carré's decision to do without Smiley and the Circus in *The Little Drummer Girl*. Its conclusion is that the introduction of a new central character, Charlie, and of a new social situation, the Israeli–Palestinian conflict, allows for an expansion of le Carré's world view, but that his frame of reference remains essentially unchanged. Thus, neither Israeli nor Palestinian society provides an environment which is any more hospitable to the pursuit of full humanity than those which appear in the earlier novels, and yet in Charlie le Carré creates a heroine who affirms even more than does Smiley the ability of the individual to persist in his quest for maturity despite the most daunting of circumstances.

Le Carré is an important writer. His vision of human experience in the context of modern society is a profound one, and he has striven throughout ten novels to develop techniques which will allow him to give it effective fictional expression. It is the aim of this book to make both the vision and its expression clear. If it is successful, whippets notwithstanding, the critical act will have proved useful.

# CHAPTER ONE

# Le Carré's Unifying Vision

S INCE THE PUBLICATION of *Call for the Dead*, John le Carré has returned again and again to the same subject matter – the affairs of the British Intelligence Headquarters in Cambridge Circus – and to the same character – George Smiley. It would be a mistake, however, for readers to limit their attention to the George Smiley espionage novels. For, important as they are in expressing le Carré's concerns, these concerns are not in any final sense tied to a single fictional world. *A Murder of Quality*, which places Smiley in a public school context, *A Small Town in Germany*, which deals with British diplomacy in Bonn, and *The Naive and Sentimental Lover*, which explores an intricate triangle of relationships between a failed novelist, his wife and a successful pram manufacturer, are informed by much the same vision of human experience as the Circus novels, *Call for the Dead*, *The Spy Who Came in from the Cold*, *The Looking-Glass War*, *Tinker, Tailor, Soldier, Spy*, *The Honourable Schoolboy*, and *Smiley's People*. The same is also true of *The Little Drummer Girl*, which examines an English actress's entanglement in the Israeli–Palestinian conflict. However, the relationship of this novel to le Carré's other works is sufficiently complex to merit separate discussion in a later chapter.

1

# I

What lends unity to le Carré's fiction is his persistent concern to explore the ways in which the individual deals with the problem of reconciling the essentially irreconcilable elements of which his personality is composed. For le Carré, human nature is constructed around the twin poles of nature and art, feeling and reason, or what he calls – thereby explicitly acknowledging his indebtedness to Schiller – the naive and the sentimental. Helen offers the following definition of the terms in *The Naive and Sentimental Lover*: 'Shamus is *naive . . . because he lives life and doesn't imitate it. Feeling is knowledge. . . . You're sentimental. . . .* You've left the natural state behind and you've become . . . part of civilization, sort of . . . corrupt. . . . What Nietzsche calls innocence, and that's what you've lost.'[1] Within this central opposition between feeling and reflection (as naive and sentimental are usually understood) is a series of conflicting terms and, as Schiller demonstrates in *The Aesthetic Education of Man*, the individual is pulled simultaneously towards multiplicity and unity, anarchy and order, spontaneity and custom, energy and harmony, the concrete and the abstract, freedom and restraint, reality and formality, the present and the universal.

Impossible though it may be ever to achieve a synthesis of the naive and sentimental aspects of the self, for both

---

[1] (London: Hodder and Stoughton, 1971), ch. VI, pp. 61–2. Further references to le Carré's novels will be cited in the text (see Abbreviations list). Because the pagination of the American editions cited on the Abbreviations page and of paperback editions (Penguin and Pan in Britain and Bantam in the USA) is different from the editions which I have used, references will cite chapter (in Roman numerals) as well as page.

Schiller and le Carré this is precisely what the individual who aspires to complete humanity must seek: 'This reciprocal relation ... is in the truest sense of the term the idea of his [Man's] humanity, and consequently something infinite to which he can approximate ever nearer in the course of time, without ever reaching it.'[2] How close he can come to the ideal depends to a considerable extent on his social situation. The struggle to reconcile feeling's anarchic impulses with reason's desire for 'moral unity'[3] becomes much easier in a society where the communal wisdom, that enshrining of the products of reason in manners, morals and institutions, has not sacrificed a sense of the complexity and multiplicity of the individual personality in its search for unity and order. As Schiller puts it: 'The State should respect not merely the objective and generic, but also the subjective and specific character of its individuals, and in extending the invisible realm of morals it must not depopulate the realm of phenomena.'[4] For him, Greek civilization in its golden age achieved this ideal: 'Combining fullness of form with fullness of content, at once philosophic and creative, at the same time tender and energetic, we see them uniting the youthfulness of fantasy with the manliness of reason in a splendid humanity'.[5]

However, neither Schiller nor le Carré believes that his own society offers the individual such a fertile environment. Schiller condemns the Europe of the late eighteenth century for its obsession with Utility, and argues that 'if the community makes function the measure of a man ... so gradually individual concrete life is extinguished, in order that the abstract life of the whole may prolong its

---

[2] Friedrich Schiller, *On the Aesthetic Education of Man,* trans. Reginald Snell (New York: Ungar, 1965), p. 73.
[3] Ibid., p. 34.
[4] Ibid., p. 32.
[5] Ibid., p. 38.

sorry existence, and the State remains eternally alien to its citizens because nowhere does feeling discover it'.[6] Contemporary British society is flawed, in le Carré's view, because it grants excessive prestige to external marks of worth such as inherited position, good manners and material possessions and affords little value to the naive impulse to live intensely in the present guided by feeling.[7] Thus, Shamus in *The Naive and Sentimental Lover* who tries to base his life on 'Impact' (*NS*, XXV, 261), his term for a direct and unrestrained meeting of human beings, remains something of a pariah while Cassidy, the successful entrepreneur who allows money and symbols of social status to mediate between him and others, is generally respected.

The failure of British society to nurture the individual's impulse towards completeness is rooted, according to le Carré, in the 'accelerated history'[8] which it has experienced during the last forty years. The Britain which he evokes in his novels has been stunned by rapid change. A way of life based on Empire, a functioning class system, and a creed of service, which seemed so secure before the Second World War, has been swept away. As Connie Sachs says of her contemporaries, the generation which came to adulthood in the 1930s, 'Poor loves. Trained to Empire, trained to rule the waves. All gone. All taken away' (*TT*, XIII, 113).

---

[6] Ibid., pp. 40–1.

[7] My discussion here focuses on the society which lies at the centre of le Carré's fictional world. However, later analyses of fictional landscape (ch. 2) and of Israeli and Palestinian societies (ch. 5) indicate that le Carré is equally sceptical about the ability of other modern societies, with the exception of Chinese Hong Kong, to help individuals in their search for balanced personalities.

[8] Le Carré used this phrase, in a radio interview with Andrew Rutherford, 'Spymaster', *Kaleidoscope*, BBC, Radio 4, 13 Sept. 1979 transcript, p. 11. Transcripts of this interview and other BBC material cited can be consulted at the BBS Script Library, The Langham, Portland Place, London.

Nothing is left in the wake of this dramatic change except the decaying remnants of once vital institutions. The class system, for all its inherent tendency to frustrate the impulse to love and communicate in a simple human way, was based originally on principles which could be traced back to some fundamental lessons taught by the emotions. Those who were picked out by birth to be leaders, whether as owners of great estates, politicians, clergymen, soldiers, sailors or Empire administrators, acquired as part of their training a sense of obligation to those further down the social scale. The lower orders, in their turn, were taught that authority should have a human face. Thus there developed an institutional parallel of the naive impulse to care for others. However, with the transfer of power from the aristocracy to the entrepreneurial class, a process completed with the loss of the last remnants of Empire after the Second World War, the class system was stripped of its paternalistic aspects. As a result a social order once based upon naive truths became merely sentimental, and the inevitable product of continuing to organize people into arbitrary groups with very different levels of power and prestige was alienation, conflict, misunderstanding and resentment. According to le Carré all attempts made since 1945 to replace the system of class privilege with a more egalitarian social framework have failed, with the result that his country's institutions are still dominated by a bigotry that 'poisons the natural communication between British men and women'.[9]

Le Carré's portrait of Carne School in A Murder of Quality offers a particularly sharp analysis of what has happened to the class system. With the decline of the traditional ruling class, the public school, an institution created to produce leaders for the 'old' model of British

---

[9] John le Carré, 'England Made Me', Observer, 13 Nov. 1977, p. 25.

society, has ceased to exercise any meaningful function. Its role, as le Carré says of Carne, is now one of 'keeping the new world out and the old world secure' (IX, 223). By continuing to indoctrinate its students with a sense of superiority, the public school simply creates a class consciousness which serves as an offensive weapon rather than the basis for a code of obligation to others. Le Carré says of his own public school, Sherborne, the model for Carne, 'We all knew who the Jews were in school and made sure they knew it too. . . . We doubled up with mirth at the sound of lower class accents. . . . We called everybody who wasn't at a private school an oik.'[10] No character in *A Murder of Quality* is more adept at this hateful game of separating 'people like ourselves' (X, 226) from the lower orders than Shane Hecht. She seeks power over George Smiley, for instance, by taunting him with her knowledge of his unfittedness for the social circles he has entered through marriage:

'The only Smiley I ever heard of married Lady Ann Sercombe at the end of the war. . . . A very curious match. I understand he was quite unsuitable. . .'. For a moment, no more, he could discern nothing but the steady gaze of Shane Hecht upon him, and knew she was waiting for an answer. And then she released him as if to say: 'I could crush you, you see. But I won't, I'll let you live'. (X, 230)

Le Carré's novels are full of similar examples of the ability of class consciousness to forestall human communication. Haldane in *The Looking-Glass War* equates class with personal worth and as a result regards the eminently decent but working-class and foreign Fred Leiser as 'a

[10] Ibid.

singularly unpleasant person': 'Common, in a Slav way. Small. He plays the Rittmeister. It's most unattractive. . . . He dresses like a bookie, but I suppose they all do that' (X, 118). The relationship between Bradfield and Turner in *A Small Town in Germany* is similarly truncated by the failure of either party to transcend the 'centuries of suspicion' (IV, 46) created by their difference in class. A first view of Turner – 'the canvas bag clutched in the heavy fist, the battered fawn suit, the unyielding, classless features' – is enough to bring the usually composed Bradfield near to expressing 'involuntary anger' (IV, 42), and Turner addresses Bradfield 'in a manner that might have been deliberately chosen to annoy' (IV, 44).

The sense of *noblesse oblige* which once lent a human dimension to the class system was reinforced by a complex code of politeness, which served as a ritual means of expressing one's acknowledgement of and willingness to serve the needs of others. However, just as the class system ceased to be an institutional embodiment of principles derived from naive impulses, so did the system of manners and in contemporary England it is at best a barrier to communication. George Smiley is repeatedly caught in situations where the demand to behave politely prevents him from expressing his feelings. He has no means at his disposal, for instance, of rebutting Lacon's assumption that they are friends and, in *Smiley's People,* finds himself committed, very much against his will, to a 'seminar' (V, 64) on marriage. At worst, when employed by characters like Shane Hecht and Roddy Martindale, polite codes become weapons of hate and thus a source of divisiveness. Shane Hecht's concern is not with the quality of her own manners but with any inadequacies in the manners of others that will help to establish their inferiority. Thus, she says of Stella Rode: 'It was the day I presented her to Lady Sawley. She wore such a *nice* little hat – the one she wore on Sundays, you know. And *so* respectful. She called her "my lady." ... Rather feudal, don't you think, dear?' (X, 228). Roddy Martindale is equally adept at reversing the traditional function of politeness. When he asks Smiley to give a message of love to Ann he is neither expressing real concern for her nor even parroting a polite formula. Rather, his intention is to link her name to his previous comment that 'women literally bow down before' (*TT*, II, 29) Bill Haydon, and to let Smiley know, in the cruellest possible way, that he is aware of his wife's infidelity.

The degeneration of the class system and of manners into mere tokens in a game of prestige does much to transform Britain into a society whose norms contradict the individual's naive impulses. This transformation is brought nearer to completion by the tendency to give increasing value to material objects. Aldo Cassidy in *The Naive and Sentimental Lover* is typically modern in that even within the privacy of his own thoughts he cannot separate himself from the things that he owns. His car functions as a 'womb' (I, 12) and is such a part of his self-image that he feels personally challenged when Shamus questions its value: 'Once again it appeared to be an examination in principle, a fundamental questioning of certain unstated values which were inherent in the car's existence, and it only added to Cassidy's unease' (II, 25). Cassidy's office plays a similar role and while in it he experiences a deep sense of security and an increase in self-esteem: 'Cassidy's office was not unlike Cassidy's car: a mahogany bastion against the non-negotiable hazards of terrestial existence. In Audley Street he was neither Aldo nor Cassidy, but *Mister Aldo,* a Christian name treated with Christian respect' (IX, 89).

When Cassidy reaches out beyond the self he allows money to mediate between him and others. He is an inveterate tipper – 'it was a very large tip but Cassidy abroad believed in laying strong fences against disrespect' (XVI, 167) – and he even introduces money into his transactions with God:

> 'It's for the fabric,' Cassidy explained. 'For rebuilding the church. It's falling down.'
> 'Jesus,' said Shamus, staring at the mute mouth of the offertory box. 'Jesus. There must be *someone* you don't pay'. (XVIII, 187)

Money plays an equally important role in all Cassidy's most intimate personal relationships. He offers his wife money for home improvements as a substitute for affection, communicates with his father by means of a monthly cheque, and writes to his son, Mark, with whom he realizes he has 'no relationship' to reassure him that '*the Children's Trust, of which you and Hug are equal beneficiaries, is made up of a wide spread of equities and gilt-edged*' (IX, 90). Even while Cassidy is struggling to break with his prescribed pattern of existence and meet Shamus and Helen on their terms, he cannot stop himself from buying them everything from flowers to a flat. Finally, he is unable to accept Helen's love without first trying to compensate Shamus financially for the loss of his wife.

Cassidy typifies a recurring figure in le Carré's novels. Oliver Lacon seeks to increase his importance by buying 'a Berkshire Camelot' (*TT,* IV, 37); Miss Peate disapproves of Alan Turner because of his shoes (*ST,* IV, 57); Leclerc believes that an official car will improve his status (*LG,* IX, 93). In fact, materialistic attitudes are so deeply ingrained that anyone who acts from other motives is liable to be the source of considerable confusion. In *A Small Town in Germany* Leo Harting's theft of secret government documents creates an apparently impenetrable mystery because no one at the British Embassy in Bonn can understand that he was motivated by love and not profit. Love for his fellow man is the source of Harting's hatred of Nazism, and love for his murdered former fiancée, Margaret Eichman, and for his present mistress, Hazel Bradfield, is what enables him to escape the prevailing 'lethargy' (XVI, 262) of his world and act decisively against the ex-Nazi, Klaus Karfeld. Drake Ko in *The Honourable Schoolboy* proves to be equally puzzling to British Intelligence because the explanation for his connection to the transfer of large sums of money into Vientiane is also to be found in love – he is trying to organize a reunion with his brother Nelson – and not, as is readily assumed, in personal gain.

So pronounced has this deviation from Schillerian social ideals become that, for le Carré, Britain now bears a clear resemblance to the world of espionage, a subculture which, as I will be showing later in the chapter, necessarily places extreme emphasis on sentimental forms of behaviour and denies value to feeling, spontaneity and individuality. The similarity is most evident in the extent to which British citizens behave like spies. For some, surveillance provides a substitute for human interaction. Thus, Mrs Yates in *The Looking-Class War* watches everyone 'night and day' (II, 21) from behind her curtains; Norman enlivens his job as a porter at the Hotel Islay by lurking outside the bedrooms of honeymooners (*TT*, XV, 126); and the newspaper editor, Stubbs, 'listened to incoming calls from correspondents without telling them he was on the line' (*HS*, V, 106). For others, a sense of security is bound up in the keeping of secrets. Thursgood, for example, is determined that Maltby's trunk will remain unopened because 'some things are best locked away' (*TT*, I, 9), and Westerby seeks to preserve the fragile stability of his relationship with his stepmother by hiding the evidence that he has broken her teacup (*HS*, V, 104). The dehumanized nature of their society has made a third group of

British people so unsure of their personal identity that they operate quite literally under cover. Among the most notable of these are Lizzie Worthington, who invents a comprehensive alternative biography (*HS*, XIII, 294) and the schoolteacher Terence Fielding in *A Murder of Quality*, who conceals a deep-seated self-loathing under a carefully constructed façade of flamboyance.

There are two other important sources of parallels between Britain's secret and overt worlds. First, le Carré's technique of symbolic description, which is discussed in chapter 2, reveals that the bleak, soulless qualities which we associate with espionage, and which are very evident in descriptions of the Circus, are equally characteristic of all other aspects of the British landscape. Second, a comparison of professions conducted later in this chapter makes it clear that naive qualities are no more valued in occupations of such central importance to British life as diplomacy and government administration that they are in espionage.

## II

The central problem in all le Carré's novels is how to be fully human in a society whose institutions have lost all connection with individual feeling. He has not yet arrived at a definitive answer and is indeed not likely to do so, for he is convinced that 'the components of life as we live it are irreconcilable, and chaotic. The art of survival is to function in spite of this.'[11] Nevertheless, as a self-confessed romantic, he is committed to seek an answer, even if it is not to be found.[12]

---

[11] Miriam Gross, 'The Secret World of John le Carré', *Observer*, 3 Feb. 1980, pp. 33–5.
[12] Le Carré admits this in a radio interview with S. W. Lambert, *The Lively Arts*, BBC Radio 3, 30 Oct. 1968, transcript, p. 2.

Le Carré's search has revealed that the problem is of such enormous proportions that, rather than attempt to come to terms with it, most people simply gravitate to one pole of reality and deny any validity to the other. Those characters in le Carré's novels who long to follow their naive impulses avoid entering into conflict with the world around them by one of three means. They either retreat into an almost mythological past where social reality is consistent with the promptings of the emotions, escape into fantasy which, in its most extreme form, becomes madness, or they simply refuse to acknowledge that there is any reality other than that created by the feelings.

A few of those who wish to live entirely in accordance with the mores of their society seem so dehumanized that they have no problems dealing with contradictory emotional demands. Most, however, must actively seek to cultivate the sentimental at the expense of the naive aspects of their personalities. This is most often achieved by entering professions such as espionage which deny any value to feeling, or government administration and diplomacy that have no place for feeling or immediate experience. The logical conclusion of this tendency to escape the naive self, as le Carré and his hero, George Smiley, are acutely aware, is the adoption of a monistic and absolutist social philosophy, such as communism, which offers a more coherent denial of feeling and immediate experience than does contemporary British society.

The pessimistic air introduced into the novels by the preponderance of escapist characters is reinforced by the tendency of those who try to grapple with all aspects of reality to fail. Characters such as Alec Leamas and Aldo Cassidy emerge from the safe havens of spying and the business world and try to follow the commands of their feelings. Both are made more whole by the experience of love that results, but neither is able to achieve a *rapproche-*

*ment* with the sentimental reality by which he was once defined and each is eventually defeated by it. Others such as Peter Guillam, Jim Prideaux and Jerry Westerby who re-enter the present after years spent under the comfortable illusion that the emotionally more satisfying world of pre-war Britain still exists, are similarly unable to survive the transition.

Of all le Carré's characters only a handful have any success in integrating the naive and sentimental aspects of the personality. The most notable are Charlie, the heroine of *The Little Drummer Girl* (discussed in chapter 5), and George Smiley. Smiley struggles throughout his career to be at once a feeling and a rational-moral human being, and to balance the conflicting claims of his love for Ann, his academic pursuits and his career as a spy. Whether he ever manages to synthesize the naive and sentimental aspects of his experience is debatable, but Smiley is successful in that he never denies the obligation to respond to a complex reality.

Given the condition of contemporary British society it is not hard to understand why so many characters in John le Carré's novels turn to the past in search of a world which allows for the expression of feeling. Aldo Cassidy, for example, is so constricted emotionally by the present that for him it seems liberating to retreat to Haverdown, a place which conjures up visions of a more rural, communal and innocent life, and to return to the Valhalla Dance Hall, where he did once experience love: 'These were the girls he could love. The girls who passed him in buses and dressed shop windows, worked for him as secretaries, peered at him from pavements as he sat in taxis, these were his nurses, his figureheads agelessly beautiful on a changing sea' (*NS*, XIII, 144). Such visions of the past, however, have little to do with Cassidy's own personal experience and offer him only momentary escape. Those characters

13

who are able to create complete alternative worlds out of the past do so by basing them either on what they once experienced themselves or, more usually, on a semi-mythological version of reality taught them in their public schools.

The members of the Department in *The Looking-Glass War* found the Second World War so completely satisfying that it remains more real to them than anything in the present. Leclerc is, for instance, ashamed that a member of his staff should live amidst a quintessentially modern landscape of 'slums with their Babel's Tower' of a new block of flats because 'this was not the society they protected' (III, 35). In contrast to the present which is complex, confusing and without obvious mission, the war was a time when 'frontiers still existed' (VI, 64) and the individual's social role was both clear and consistent with naive impulses. The common faith was 'patriotism' (IV, 64), the commonly accepted task was to defeat the Nazi enemy, and this provided opportunities for purposeful and immediate action and the emotional satisfaction of the 'spontaneous goodwill' (II, 25) felt for each other by the Department's agents. The simplicity and clarity of the wartime situation make it analogous to the ideal world of childhood, and when Avery looks at photographs of the period he sees in them 'boys' with 'sobriquets from children's magazines: Jacko, Shorty, Pip and Lucky Joe ... and ... sunny, boyish smile[s]' (II, 25).

Equally divorced from the present are those characters, such as Jim Prideaux, Peter Guillam and Jerry Westerby, who continue to believe that the world operates according to standards taught them by their public schools. This version of reality, if it ever existed outside the pages of schoolboy fiction, has certainly ceased to be by the time Prideaux, Guillam and Westerby become adults. However, because of its compatibility with their natural inclinations

14

as 'heartfelt' (*TT*, XXIX, 254) men, they cling to it. The public school code bridges the gap between the naive and the sentimental by teaching that those simple human impulses towards fair play and loyalty should provide the basis not only for one's conduct on the cricket field but also for one's adult relationships and social role. The influence of this ethic is particularly evident in the intensely loyal masculine friendships that each man cultivates – Prideaux with Haydon, Guillam with Haydon and Smiley, and Westerby with 'old George' Smiley (*HS*, XVIII, 447). The most remarkable, both for its longevity and its fidelity, is Prideaux's relationship with Haydon. From 1938 when he takes on the role of Dobbin by helping to hang paintings for Haydon's one man exhibition, Prideaux is unfailing in his friendship until their last meeting in 1974, prior to Operation Testify, when he tries to warn Haydon of Control's madness. As Smiley remarks to himself: 'He came to warn you . . . because he loved you. To warn you. . . . Jim was watching your back for you right till the end' (*TT*, XXXVII, 343).

A continued belief in the efficacy of the public-school view of the world also underlies Prideaux, Guillam and Westerby's attitudes to their social roles as secret agents. All choose this career because they see it as a way of serving their country which, as they would have been taught at school, should be the goal of any gentleman. Guillam is thus motivated by 'a notion of English calling' and 'plain, heroic standards' (*TT*, XXXVI, 328) to give all his 'conscious loyalties' (*TT*, XI, 80) to the Circus. Since they have also thoroughly absorbed the public-school notion that England is the 'best place in the whole damn world!' (*TT*, I, 17), it never occurs to any of them to doubt the correctness of this total commitment. Prideaux's interpretation of the contemporary political situation is one that would have been shared by most products of the public schools in his generation: 'To the west, America ... full of greedy fools fouling up their inheritance. To the east, China–Russia, he drew no distinction: boiler suits, prison camps and a damn long march to nowhere.' (*TT*, I, 17). Westerby is equally convinced that '*we* were right' (*HS*, XVIII, 447).

Decisive action comes easily to men from whom social values and individual needs coincide so readily. When Control asks Prideaux, in schoolboy terminology cynically chosen to appeal to his public-school morality, to seek out the 'rotten apple' (*TT*, XXXI, 269) in the barrel, he obeys without hesitation although he cannot bring himself to believe that there could be a traitor in British intelligence. Guillam suffers through a disappointing career marred by 'his butchered agents in Morocco, his exile to Brixton, the daily frustration of his efforts' (*TT*, XXXVI, 328), and yet he responds at once to the call to help Smiley unmask the mole, Gerald. Westerby is so certain of the rightness of what he is doing that he returns without question when summoned from retirement by the Circus and at his briefing asks of Smiley only that 'You point me and I'll march' (*HS*, V, 115).

Prideaux, Guillam and Westerby are, then, stranded in the past and, fated as they are to remain perpetual 'honourable schoolboys,'[13] each is characterized by a quality of childlike innocence very like that expressed by the war-time photographs in Leclerc's office. The boys at Thursgood's school recognize in Jim Prideaux a companion rather than a teacher and for Smiley, Jim makes 'the night landscape ... suddenly innocent; it was like a great canvas on which nothing bad or cruel had ever been painted' (*TT*, XXXII, 287–8). Peter Guillam, although in his forties, reminds Smiley of 'an undergraduate sculling

[13] See le Carré, 'Enġland Made Me', p. 25.

on the river' (*TT*, IV, 35) and is habitually addressed by Alleline as 'young Peter Guillam' (*TT*, XXI, 175). The Tuscan villagers perceive a similar quality in Westerby with his book sack, his 'bashful and enthusiastic' air, his vocabulary full of words like 'gosh, super', and give him the nickname of 'the schoolboy' (*HS*, II, 38).

The temptation to step backwards in time in search of a simpler and emotionally more satisfying version of reality is clearly very great. The problem is, of course that whether they realize it or not these 'children' are living in the same complex and disappointing world as the rest of us. In this context innocence has a disturbing way of becoming immaturity, and its possessors become victims or monsters, thus transforming their 'dream' (*LG*, XXII, 236) into nightmare. When Operation Mayfly restores the Department to operational status Leclerc simply assumes that the conditions of the Second World War have miraculously resurfaced. Former comrades, Fred Leiser and Jack Johnson, are called back into active service, training sessions take place in Oxford as they did during the war, and the training itself is based on old techniques and equipment. What Leclerc cannot see is that things are not as they were. Leiser is no longer a young man, advances in radio technology have made their equipment obsolete, and worst of all, there has been a dramatic shift in values. The patriotism and universal goodwill which united the British against the Nazis no longer exist and it turns out that Control of the Circus, far from helping the Department against the East German enemy, is in fact plotting its downfall. Brought face to face with contemporary reality, the fabric of fantasy created by the Department inevitably dissolves. Once he is sent into East Germany Leiser the agent is transformed from hero to victim and all, except Leclerc who has retreated into insanity rather than face up to the monstrosity of what he has done, wake 'from a

17

single dream' (LG, XXII, 236). The definitive metaphor for the insubstantiality of the Department's world of illusion is provided by Fred Leiser in the moments before his arrest: 'I went for a walk, once, it was raining and there was this man by the river, drawing on the pavement in the rain. Fancy that! Drawing with chalk in the rain, and the rain just washing it away' (LG, XXIII, 245).

Whereas others become the victims of Leclerc's attempt to borrow 'an ethic from the past and [apply] it to the future',[14] the illusions of Prideaux, Guillam and Westerby usually harm no one but themselves.[15] Experience does little to penetrate Prideaux's blindness. Neither Control's warning that there is a traitor in the ranks of the Circus nor the evidence of betrayal provided by his own capture during Operation Testify does anything to lessen his faith in British decency. Prideaux even boasts to Karla during his interrogation by the Russians of the superiority of British Intelligence, making the traitor, Haydon, his unfortunate choice of example: 'If you had one Bill Haydon in your damned outfit, you could call it set and match' (TT, XXXII, 285). Smiley's later attempt to lead Prideaux to see the implications of his experiences simply fails to elicit any response: 'The discursive, almost chatty tone with which Smiley threw out these theories found no resonance in Jim' (TT, XXXII, 286). The consequences of Prideaux's failure to close the gap between his vision of the Circus and its reality is his own consistent victimization. The mission into Czechoslovakia leaves him crippled by a wound in the back and, after his repatriation, he is cast off

[14] 'The Fictional World of Espionage', interview with Leigh Crutchley, Listener, 75 (14 April 1966), p. 549.
[15] Le Carré comments in his interview with Rutherford that characters such as Prideaux and Westerby who have 'foreshortened their critical faculties ... always get the worst drubbing in the story because you simply cannot cease to criticise.' See 'Spymaster' (transcript, p. 10).

by the Circus with no better prospects for the future than a career as a temporary teacher in minor prep. schools.

Guillam and Westerby are similarly victimized by their commitment to an outmoded vision of British institutions. For Guillam, the Circus represents all that is best in British life – loyalty, comradeship, chivalry, aristocratic grace, a spirit of adventure, plain heroic standards – and he bases his entire faith on its 'magic' (*TT*, XXXVI, 328). His only involvement outside his career is with a 'network of girlsfriends' (*TT*, XI, 80); otherwise he expects the Circus to meet all his emotional needs. However, the reality of the Circus is very different from Guillam's fantasy and it fails to give him the personal or professional fulfilment he seeks. His career as a field agent ends in disaster when Haydon betrays his networks to the Russians, and his subsequent attempts to be of service at home are frustrated when he is 'shoved out to grass in Brixton' after 'Alleline's crowd' come to power simply 'because he had the wrong connections, among them Smiley' (*TT*, XI, 80). Guillam does experience some of the satisfaction of real comradeship as a result of his long professional association with George Smiley, and there is perhaps something genuine in his bond with Bill Haydon, despite the central lie upon which it is based. However, such relationships are the exception rather than the rule. For most of Guillam's colleagues the Circus is a network of rivalries, a 'cauldron of male hates',[16] rather than an extension of the public-school model of masculine friendship. Thus, people like Alleline mistrust Guillam because of his connections with the Control-Smiley faction and Lauder Strickland despises him because of his lowly position in the Circus hierarchy.

---

[16] The phrase is Arthur Hopcraft's. See 'How Smiley Came to Life: John le Carré Traces the History of Alec Guinness's Television Role', *Telegraph Sunday Magazine*, 21 Oct. 1977, p. 111.

Westerby fares no better than Guillam. The Circus is everything to him: at the social level it provides an opportunity to fulfil his aristocratic sense of responsibility and at the personal, it provides a surrogate father in the shape of George Smiley. Therefore, like Guillam, he is prepared to put the Circus before any other aspect of his life. Although the relationship he forms in Tuscany with the orphan promises him more emotional satisfaction than any of his many marriages, Westerby abandons her immediately when the Circus, under the significant code name of 'guardian', calls him back to London. Westerby's reward for his loyalty to an institution which is not at all what he imagines is to be exploited repeatedly. For his accurate but unwelcome information about Operation Testify, he is first abused by Toby Esterhase and then cast aside. During Operation Dolphin, he is used, not as he fantasizes, as one of 'St George's children go[ing] forth to save the empire' (*HS*, VI, 124) but as the exploiter of innocent people such as Frost, Luke, Lizzie Worthington and Drake Ko.

The final stage in the process of victimization for Prideaux, Guillam and Westerby is, as was the case in *The Looking-Glass War*, the inevitable realization of the insubstantiality of the world they have created. Prideaux suffers anguish when the unmasking of Haydon finally forces him to admit not only that the service is corrupt but that he has been betrayed by his lifelong friend. The same incident is responsible for Guillam's disillusionment and has similar painful, personal implications because Haydon is in many ways the cornerstone of his faith in the purity of the Circus: 'Haydon was more than his model, he was his inspiration, the torch-bearer of a certain kind of antiquated romanticism, a notion of English calling which – for the very reason that it was vague and understated and elusive – had made sense of Guillam's life till now' (*TT*, XXXVI, 328). For Westerby, disillusionment is more gradual but equally painful. The pattern of betrayal in which Operation Dolphin involves him finally becomes so insistent that Westerby is forced to admit that, far from pursuing an ideal of service to others, he is involved in a way of life in which 'the paying is actually done by the other poor sods' (HS, XX, 489).

The Looking-Glass War terminates at this moment of enlightenment but le Carré clearly suggests that, once robbed of their illusions, his characters have little future. Fred Leiser is, of course, destined for execution by the East Germans, Avery appears to have been broken by the experience, and Leclerc survives only by going mad. Although Prideaux, Guillam and Westerby are not eliminated so ruthlessly from future consideration, le Carré does not offer in these cases much more hope that lives, based for so long on illusion, can be remade. Haydon's exposure does have a liberating effect on Guillam at first. He is no longer forced to look beyond the confines of the once sacrosanct Circus for the source of his emotional confusion. As a result he is able to free his girlfriend, Camilla, 'from the toils of doublecross to which he had latterly consigned her' and invest his emotional energy in penetrating some of the real 'mystery' (TT, XXXVII, 333) she poses for him. However, it does not seem that Guillam has much success in his subsequent attempts to live maturely and to satisfy his naive impulses through sexual relationships rather than the Circus. Following his affairs with Camilla and Molly Meakin, he marries a 'child bride', the supremely silly Marie-Claire who, with her 'awful notepaper with its grazing bunnies' (SP, XVIII, 226) and her fond wish that she might minister to a sick Guillam from her supply of 'invalid foods' (SP, XVIII, 225), seems to be nothing more than an alternative outlet for the anachronistic chivalry and romanticism he once invested in the Circus.

Westerby also responds to his disenchantment with the

Circus by seeking a new outlet for his naive impulses. Freed at last from his attempt to live in an idealized past, he decides that it is 'high time ... that you were present at certain ... crucial moments in your history' (*HS*, XVIII, 451), by which he means that he intends to pursue Lizzie Worthington rather than obey the Circus's order that he return to London. However, the thrust towards immediate experience contained within this resolution turns out to be illusory, for Westerby simply approaches Lizzie in the archaic spirit of romance and schoolboy adventure that characterized his relationship with the Circus. He imagines 'carting [her] away on his white charger' (*HS*, XVIII, 450), and pursues his 'Galahad act' (*HS*, XX, 477) so single-mindedly that he is killed while trying to do his 'Tarzan stuff' (*HS*, XXI, 516) in her defence.

Of the three, Jim Prideaux might seem to be the most successful in surviving disillusionment. He revenges himself on Haydon by breaking his neck and, after a period of mourning, picks up the threads of his life at Thursgood's school, where he can look to friendships with boys like Jumbo Roach as an outlet for his ability to care. However, what le Carré is in fact offering in Prideaux is a portrait of a man who, like Leclerc, cannot escape his commitment to an anachronistic vision of experience despite the intrusion of contemporary reality. In this instance, however, perhaps because he has such affection for the character, le Carré creates a fantasy of his own in which a man like Prideaux is able to survive and remain sane. When he kills Haydon, Prideaux is simply continuing to act in accordance with the standards of heroic schoolboy fiction, which allow for such extreme measures in the case of betrayal by a friend or lover. That he goes unpunished suggests that le Carré's novel is also operating temporarily within the conventions of such fiction. Le Carré completes his excursion into fantasy by finding for Jim the one corner of contemporary society which functions by standards similar to his own. This is of course the childhood world of Thursgood's school where Prideaux is recognized as, and admired for being, 'a stag ... something noble' (*TT*, I, 12) and is acknowledged as the living embodiment of an adventure-story character. Those same boys who can transform the debris of a failed swimming-pool project into 'an open-cast silver mine ... or a Romano-British fort' have no trouble in recognizing that Jim's hat has a 'rakish piratical curl' (I, 11) and that his 'moustache washed into fangs' (I, 12) by the rain, is like Fu Manchu's. Jim survives by becoming almost literally a boy living in a boy's world – he even tells parents that he and Roach 'were new boys together' (XXXVII, 349).

Few readers would object to le Carré's refusal in this instance to carry his analysis through to its logical con-clusion, but it would be a mistake to let this divert us from his central point. In his presentation of the Department in *The Looking-Glass War* and of the careers of Peter Guillam and Jerry Westerby, le Carré insists repeatedly that, appealing as it may be to retreat into the past in search of a social reality consistent with one's naive impulses, to do so is ultimately a self-destructive exercize.

Another way of escaping the complex modern problem of reconciling the naive and the sentimental is simply to deny that any reality exists beyond that which the feelings can define. By making such a total commitment to the naive aspects of the personality, characters such as Ann Smiley, Shamus, Camilla and the orphan reaffirm the qualities often neglected in a society that places little value on the products of spontaneous individuality. Neverthe-less, le Carré makes it clear that such people come no nearer to complete humanity than those who seek refuge in the past.

This group of characters is, as Ann says of herself,

'lawless' (*SP*, XII, 134). Their entire concern is with their own feelings and they refuse to acknowledge any guide to conduct other than that provided by an inner voice crying 'I want, I want' (*CD*, XIV, 116). Thus Smiley comments of Ann's refusal to respect the monogamy imposed by marriage: 'it was as useless to expect fidelity of Ann as of this tiny shepherdess in her glass case' (*CD*, XIV, 110). Shamus is equally convinced of the sovereignty of his feelings and advises Cassidy '*Never regret, never apologise. ... Live without heed to the consequences ... give everything for today and not a damn for tomorrow ... those who are afraid make rules*' (*NS*, XXVII, 293). This rejection of 'technique' (that is, forms of behaviour that are learned rather than spontaneous) as a 'compromise with reality' (*TT*, XI, 92) can lead to a clarity of vision denied those who are too caught up in social reality. Characters who are guided by their naive impulses are often able to act decisively in accordance with the needs of the moment, as when Camilla immediately accepts Guillam's unexpected proposal that they become lovers, and they have a full appreciation of the power of love as the most important feeling. As Shamus says, 'Love is the bridge between what we *are* and what we can *become*' (*NS*, XXXVI, 385). The orphan displays a similar understanding of the significance attached to love when she demands of Westerby, as a condition of getting in his bed, 'Just never lie to me. . . . No words, no lies. Got it?' (*HS*, II, 48).

However, despite all that can be achieved by granting sovereignty to the feelings, le Carré is not at all convinced of the ultimate wisdom of refusing the guidance not only of social convention, that is, of the institutionalized products of reason, but also of reason itself. For le Carré, life does not exist 'only in excess' (*NS*, XVII, 179), as Shamus affirms, but in a constant search for 'moderation' (*TT*, XXIII, 207), a term he derives from Schiller who employs it in talking of the need to establish a balance between the naive and sentimental aspects of the self.[17]

One of the major disadvantages of living entirely in accordance with the demands of the feelings is that the individual is liable to become solipsistic and seek not truth but self-indulgence. While restraint and concern with social convention can end in 'imprisonment of the soul' (*NS*, XVIII, 198), it can also be part of the humanizing process involved in recognizing the unique existence of others. Ranging from Camilla's trivial rudeness in playing her flute in the early hours of the morning because 'she didn't give a damn about the neighbours' (*TT*, XI, 91), to Ann's repeated sexual betrayals of Smiley, le Carré's committedly naive characters frequently offend against this humane ideal: '*I love you, I hate you, I need you.* Such apocalyptic statements reminded him of Ann when she had run out of money or love. The heart of the sentence is the subject, he thought. It is not the verb, least of all the object. It is the ego, demanding its feed' (*SP*, IV, 43). Thus, when Cassidy invokes the public-school code and judges Shamus a 'bully' for trying to seduce Hall's girlfriend, Sal, he is not merely being pompous but is offering a valid critique of his friend's approach to experience by placing it in a moral context:

> At Sherborne, Shamus, we called it bullying.
> We may not have had a very high opinion of *ourselves* ... but we did, I think, respect one another. ... That, it seems to me, Shamus, is the definition of a reasonable man. ...
> A *bully* is someone who picks on those who are weaker than himself. ... A *bully* performs acts of brutality against those who cannot retaliate. ...

---

[17] Schiller, *Aesthetic Education*, p. 72.

So I'm afraid, Shamus, we do not approve. Sal may be a slut. Conceded. But Hall was your friend. He loved you and he loved Sal, and that's why he didn't hit you. (*NS*, XXVII, 292)

The second problem for people who follow only the dictates of feeling is that, like those who try to live in the past, they are liable to be victimized by the very codes which they try to ignore. In Shamus's case the victimization results from a failure entirely to discount social standards. For all his mockery of 'Gerrards Crosser[s]' and 'disguised Bishops' (VI, 57), he is in fact concerned with how such people judge him. Shamus is at times, for example, anxious to be accepted on Cassidy's terms and has aspirations to be a successful pram salesman. However, he never fully admits to himself this concern with the opinions of the 'Many-too-Many' (VI, 58) and so is unequipped to deal with any negative judgements they make of him. The rejection of his novel, for instance, hits hard at Shamus's self-esteem and brings him close to despair: '"All right," Shamus whispered, letting him loose as the tears came, "all right, lover. If I'm so bloody marvellous, why did you turn down my novel?"' (*NS*, XXI, 227).

Others, such as the orphan, who are completely indifferent to social convention, are nevertheless vulnerable to its influence. Thus, her affair with Westerby, to which she committed herself without regard for anything but the pursuit of love, is brought to an end because Westerby retains a sense of social obligation and abandons her when the Circus summons him back from retirement. Her suffering is intense: 'she was trembling and her face had turned white and ill. . . . When he tried to kiss her, she was cold as marble, so he let her be. At night they slept together and it was worse than being alone' (*HS*, II, 50).

The third way which le Carré explores of preserving the naive self from the threats posed to it by the nature of contemporary British society is through escape into fantasy or madness. Fantasy offers Aldo Cassidy, for example, opportunities to give expression to the emotions and impulses so carefully suppressed in his life as a businessman and middle-class husband. Visits to the cinema, with its images of 'a dark-haired girl in period costume [who] will unbutton her blouse in French' (NS, II, 25), satisfy in part the need for unrestrained sexuality that goes unfulfilled in his tame marriage to a woman whose nipples remind him of 'frozen pips' (XI, 120). Besides taking advantage of the fantasies offered in films, Cassidy creates a number of his own. At one time he imagines himself to be a philanthropist buying land for sports-fields and at another becoming a socialist member of parliament. Although different in detail, these alternative biographies all serve the function of providing Cassidy with a role that offers a social outlet for his naive longing to make purposeful contact with other people, something which is lacking in his career as a pram manufacturer, the only point of which is profit.

Whereas Cassidy moves in and out of his fantasies, Lizzie Worthington in *The Honourable Schoolboy* lives almost entirely in an invented version of reality that allows her far more spiritual and emotional scope than do her real social circumstances, as the daughter of a retired Post Office employee and the wife of an Islington schoolteacher. Through the power of her imagination Lizzie transforms even the most mundane or sordid circumstances into something 'glamorous' (XIII, 302) and exciting. She thinks of her parents, not as lower-middle-class people eking out a dull retirement at 7 Arcady Mansions with its 'cramped view of the ninth green' (X, 227), but as aristocratic fox hunters living in 'the usual tumble-down

27

schloss in Shropshire' (XIII, 294). The scar on her chin, really inflicted by a drunken lover, becomes in her mind the result of a hunting accident. Lizzie also makes gold out of the dross of her seedy life in the east. Fantasy transforms 'selling kegs of unbranded whisky to American layabouts' (X, 234), going 'behind the hedge with half of Asia' (X, 238), living and working in abject poverty with the pilots Tiny Ricardo and Charlie Marshall, and acting as an informant to Sam Collins, into 'fabulous adventure[s]' (XIII, 302); she imagines herself to have 'owned and managed one of the major distilling concessions in that wartorn country' (X, 234), to have been a 'pioneer' (XIII, 303) of air travel and to have served as a 'senior and respected operative of our British Intelligence' (X, 235) who risks death to do 'good Work' for 'the Country' (X, 236).

Lizzie Worthington's fantasy life is much more complete than Aldo Cassidy's. Only occasionally, and then under the influence of alcohol, does Cassidy lose sight of the distinction between illusion and reality. Lizzie Worthington, on the other hand, is close to believing in her fantasies and even adopts a new name – Liese Worth – which she feels is more appropriate to the new reality she has created for herself. Clearly, she is close to the borderline where fantasy crosses over into madness. However, the struggle to alter social reality so that it conforms to her emotional urges never quite leads Lizzie across that borderline, as it does Tatiana, also known as Alexandra, in *Smiley's People*. Tatiana experiences a more intense conflict between the definitions of reality offered by her feelings and by her society than any other character in le Carré's novels. As a motherless child, her main naive impulse is to love her father, the Russian agent, Karla; yet, as a member of Russian society she does not have a father because Karla has been forced to disown her to protect his own social position, following the ideological disgrace of her mother. She sums up her position thus: 'Tatiana is the daughter of a man who is too important to exist' (XXVI, 315). The paradox is unbearable and Tatiana escapes into the fantasy of total self-annihilation: 'After Mother Felicity's arrival, Alexandra had held the white bed sheet to her eyes and decided that time was not passing at all, that she was in a child's white limbo where everything was shadowless, even Alexandra, even Tatiana' (XXII, 262).

Like the other forms of escapism already discussed, fantasy and madness are ultimately ineffective as ways of sidestepping the problems posed by society. Not even the most powerful imagination can actually change the nature of things, and the individual who refuses to see the world as it really is simply invites exploitation. Lizzie Worthington, for example, cannot do anything to stop her victimization by Tiny Ricardo, who beats and prostitutes her, because to acknowledge that this is what is happening would destroy her fantasy of him as a dashing hero and her special lover. Dealing with Lizzie is, as Westerby acknowledges, 'like stealing from a blind beggar. . . . She shouldn't be let loose' (HS, XIII, 293). Tatiana is even more vulnerable, because once she withdraws from engagement with the world she loses all power to act independently and is entirely subject to the wishes of others. As an ironic consequence, she becomes confined within an institution that specifically denies any value to the very impulse to love that she sought to protect by her retreat into madness: 'love was not, was not, was *not* on the curriculum' (SP, XXII, 263).

### III

In some cases, then, the naive self is so powerful that characters like Jim Prideaux, Ann Smiley and Lizzie

Worthington try, in their different ways, to deny any reality to a society whose values discourage the individual from following the guidance of feelings. Other characters when faced with the same dichotomy between the naive and the sentimental, take the opposite tack and sacrifice self to society. For some, the process of socialization is so complete that little real choice seems involved in this decision. Roddy Martindale, for instance, appears to experience no impulse to live intensely, to feel any but the pettiest emotions, or to acknowledge the humanity of those around him. His natural medium is gossip, the only thing apart from food which 'could ... move him ... deeply' (*TT*, II, 27), because at this level of discourse he can deny people any selfhood that falls beyond their class, manners, professional status, appearance and the least admirable aspects of their behaviour. However, there are few Roddy Martindales in le Carré's world and in most cases the decision to put one's faith entirely in the sentimental aspects of experience derives not from lack of feeling but from a desire to escape feelings that have proven to be a troublesome burden.

Le Carré's spies are misfits, men whose emotions have been stunted by lack of love in childhood or twisted by unsuccessful adult heterosexual relationships. Westerby and Alan Turner are, for instance, permanently distressed by their failure to draw close to their fathers. In Westerby's case this distress manifests itself in a tendency to transform powerful male figures, whether they be his old friend George Smiley or Drake Ko, the targets of his espionage activities, into substitute fathers. Ko thus appears to Westerby to be the genuine version of what his father strove to be: 'Except there was a hint – some men have it, it is like a tension: headwaiters, doormen, journalists can spot it at a glance; old Sambo *almost* had it – there was a hint of resources instantly available' (*HS*, VII, 163).

Turner's needs are almost as pressing and even brief exposure to the paternalistic Arthur Meadowes is enough to spark off a nostalgic longing for such a figure in his own life: 'That's what it would be like, he thought, to have a father you believed in: values for their own sake and a gap as wide as the Atlantic' (*ST,* VI, 90). Both men suffer further because of their failure to make marriage a compensation for lack of early emotional fulfillment. In contrast to his ability to create long-lasting male relationships, Westerby goes from wife to wife, never finding what he wants, and Turner is haunted by memories of his wife's desertion in favour of a man with superior sexual technique and perhaps more emotional warmth: 'he heard her laughing as his own wife had laughed: Alan darling, you're supposed to take me, not fight me. It's rhythm, it's like dancing, can't you understand? And Tony's such a *beautiful* dancer' (*ST,* IX, 147).

As spies, both Turner and Westerby as well as other refugees from the battleground of marriage, such as Leamas, Esterhase and Smiley, are freed from the need to continue their desperate struggle for emotional satisfaction. Turner is particularly conscious that once he begins to function as a spy he is no longer required to feel, and makes his creed, 'unreason will be your downfall. Make order out of chaos' (*ST,* IX, 150). The intensity of Turner's need to remain within such limits is indicated by his hostile reaction to anyone who strays beyond them. He rebukes Bradfield for using 'emotive terms' when describing Leo Harting because 'they put me off' (IV, 53), and furiously attacks Gaunt for allowing his friendship with Harting to interfere with security: 'Sign the night book, did he? . . . Or didn't you bloody well bother? Well, not right really, is it? You can't come over all official, not to a guest' (V, 80).

The spy strips feelings of value, however, not just by avoiding them in himself but by exploiting them in others.

31

To feel in the world of espionage is to be vulnerable. Thus, after years of carefully preserving his cover, Polyakov exposes himself to the Circus as the Russian agent, Colonel Gregor Viktorov, because he cannot resist the emotionally inspired temptation to honour his dead war-time colleagues by wearing his medals on Remembrance Day. Similarly, Frost's willingness to befriend Westerby simply means, according to the ethics of espionage, that he is a suitable target for blackmail. However, the most dramatic example in le Carré's novels of the vulnerability of the feeling individual occurs in *Smiley's People* when, by revealing his intense love for his daughter, Tatiana, Karla at last gives British Intelligence a weapon with which to defeat him.

As a substitute for the complex and often confusing guidance provided by the instinctive urge to love and to be affectionate, the spy learns to operate entirely in accordance with a set of techniques called tradecraft, which he is taught during his training at Sarratt. When Westerby sets out to blackmail Frost during Operation Dolphin, he does not act as a complex human being but shrinks comfortably into the guise of 'Sarratt man and nothing else' (*HS*, VI, 125). At dangerous moments he relies on 'his twenty years of tradecraft' (VI, 125) and any other considerations are 'blanked out' (VI, 140). His only goal is the successful completion of the operation and 'the rest of what he felt was of no account' (VI, 141). In this way the sentimental approach to experience excludes the naive.

Commitment to a way of life based on tradecraft provides the spy with a sense of order and security lacking in the chaotic realm of emotional experience. However, for le Carré, to deny feeling is finally as self-destructive as it is to live entirely through the feelings. In fact, to be completely sentimental can have precisely the same consequences as to be entirely naive because in both cases refusal to deal with all aspects of reality makes the individual subject to exploitation. The problem for people who rely entirely on technique is that they become predictable and hence vulnerable. In *Call for the Dead,* for instance, George Smiley is first able to identify and then to manipulate the future behaviour of his East German opponent Dieter Frey because he is still using the operational methods with which Smiley became familiar when they worked together during the Second World War. Similarly, the many tactics employed by Khalil in *The Little Drummer Girl* to evade Israeli intelligence come to nothing because failure to vary his bomb-making technique, with its characteristic method of tying up excess wire into a doll shape, means that he leaves behind a recognizable 'signature' (XIX, 318) which enables Kurtz to follow his progress and eventually pinpoint his location.

However, there is another and even more significant way in which the satisfaction offered by a life in espionage turns out to be false. The person ultimately most fully exploited is the spy himself because he experiences dehumanization. This tendency is epitomized by Control, the head of the Circus. Just as he has substituted for his real name one describing his function, so Control has yielded up all human considerations to the pursuit of successful technique. As he puts it himself, 'in our world we pass so quickly out of the register of hate or love' (*SC*, II, 22). In his management of operations he shows a complete disregard for any kind of human considerations and is as ready to betray his own side as the enemy. In *The Spy Who Came in from the Cold,* he not only deceives his own man, Alec Leamas, but also callously sacrifices the innocent civilian, Liz Gold, and in *The Looking-Glass War* he strands a British agent in East Germany simply to ensure the Circus's ascendency over Leclerc's department. A similarly dehumanized attitude is revealed by Toby Esterhase

33

who 'would put the dogs on his own mother' (*TT*, XI, 85); Haldane, who says of the deserted agent, Fred Leiser, 'We sent him because we needed to; we abandon him because we must' (*LG*, XXII, 238–9) and Martello who considers Jerry Westerby to be nothing more than 'a rogue elephant' (*HS*, XXI, 498) who should be shot.

For those who have committed themselves entirely to espionage as a way of escaping the demands of feeling this process of dehumanization seems almost irreversible. One character who does come to recognize the trap in which he has caught himself is Alec Leamas, but like those who eventually come to understand the illusions involved in shaping the world entirely according to the demands of feeling, he is unsuccessful in reordering his life. Leamas is almost an archetype of the cynical secret agent. For him spying serves as a refuge from a failed marriage, and he dismisses love as a 'fairy tale' (*SC*, V, 41). However, involvement with Liz Gold gives Leamas for the first time, 'the caring about little things – the faith in ordinary life; that simplicity that made you break up a bit of bread into a paper bag, walk down to the beach and throw it to the gulls' (*SC*, X, 93). Unfortunately, his response to this growth in awareness is not to seek a better balance between the demands of the naive and the sentimental, but to reject all compromise and concern with technique and to pledge himself entirely to love. Thus, when Liz Gold falls victim to Control's trap, Leamas is left only with the heroic but futile gesture of sacrificing himself also.

Government administration and diplomacy are careers which remove the individual even further from the realm of the naive than does spying. Not only are qualities like love, warmth and spontaneity considered irrelevant by the bureaucrat and diplomat but they also eschew any genuine involvement with experience. Maston, the professional civil servant, is completely unsuited to his role as head of the intelligence service because for him 'experience, perception, common sense ... were not the organs of fact. Paper was fact, Ministers were fact, Home Secretaries were hard fact', and the ultimate truth lies in 'policy' (*CD*, V, 43).

A similar state of affairs exists in diplomatic circles, and Alan Turner, the outsider for whom the Bonn Embassy is a 'dream box' (*ST*, XIII, 209), has to establish clear distinctions between 'reality' and 'diplomacy' (XII, 196). The goal of the diplomat, as Bradfield readily admits, is to maintain certain illusions: 'I'm a great believer in hypocrisy. It's the nearest we ever get to virtue. It's a statement of what we ought to be. Like religion, like art, like the law, like marriage. I serve the appearance of things' (*ST*, XVII, 286). Protocol stands alongside hypocrisy as a way of protecting the diplomat from direct experience. Life at the Bonn Embassy is, for instance, constructed around rituals in which no one believes but to which everyone adheres. The daily Chancery meeting is like 'morning prayers in an agnostic community: though contributing little in the way of inspiration or instruction, it set a tone for the day, served as a roll-call and imparted a sense of corporate activity' (*ST*, II, 12). On Sundays, the Chancery meeting is replaced by an even more pointless ritual. In an age of atheism and espoused egalitarianism, the members of the Embassy continue to file into their chapel in an order defined by their seniority in the diplomatic service: the senior wife present, 'with a little gesture of surprise, climbs the steps ahead of them and disappears through the green curtain, leaving her inferiors to follow, quite by accident, the order of succession which protocol, had they cared about such things, would exactly have demanded' (II, 24). For Bradfield, although 'theoretically a Roman Catholic', to attend Chapel is an 'iron duty' and 'a matter on which he declined to consult either his Church or his conscience' (II, 25).

The individual committed to a career in government

administration or diplomacy in which the 'destination [is] irrelevant' (*ST*, II, 16) is, like the spy, in danger of becoming dehumanized. For bureaucrats such as Maston or Oliver Lacon the object of existence is reduced to the pursuit of personal advancement. Maston is described as 'apologetically extending his empire and regretfully moving to even larger offices' (*CD*, I, 14) and Sam Collins says of Lacon: 'All power corrupts but some must govern and in that case Brother Lacon will reluctantly scramble to the top of the heap' (*TT*, XXVI, 218). Other human beings become mere tokens to be moved around according to the needs of this quest for power. Maston is willing to ignore evidence that Samuel Fennan was murdered because to acknowledge it promises little personal advantage. Similarly, Lacon colludes in Smiley's replacement as head of the Circus by Saul Enderby, at the end of Operation Dolphin, because he believes that the closer links with the Americans thereby produced will advance his own career.

For le Carré, the ultimate flaw in attempting to deny reality to the realm of feeling is that a completely dehumanized social system will result. Thus, in an interview with Leigh Crutchley, he warns that, although their goal is to protect a way of life based on individual freedom, the tactics employed by the British Government and Intelligence during the Cold War are liable to produce a society very like that of the communist enemy, in which 'sentiment' is considered to cloud 'perception', love is regarded as decadent (*SC*, XXII, 193) and in which the individual's 'humanity and courage' (*SP*, I, 23) are consistently misused: 'In the cold war we are already doing something *in fact* which I believe we are already doing *in principle* elsewhere – that is to say we are sacrificing the individual in our battle against the collective.'[18]

[18] Le Carré, 'The Fictional World of Espionage', p. 548.

## IV

Le Carré's analysis of the relationship between the individual and society in twentieth-century Britain is in many ways, then, a pessimistic one. However, despite the failure of contemporary British institutions to aid citizens in the inherently difficult task of balancing contradictory claims, le Carré refuses to yield up his faith in the individual's capacity to achieve full humanity. Mendel, for instance, as the haven of caring he creates in his semi-detached house in Mitcham suggests, is successful in maintaining a core of humanity despite the demands of his careers as CID officer and occasional spy. Charlie's achievement, as I will be arguing in my later analysis of *The Little Drummer Girl*, is even more considerable in that, as a result of the education she receives in the theatre of the real, she adds knowledge of feeling to the ability to feel and is thereby able to sustain a complex adult emotional involvement. However, the main burden of le Carré's belief in the persistence, even in the most unfavourable circumstances, of the human urge for completeness is borne by George Smiley who appears, usually at the centre, in all but three of his novels.

Awareness of what it means to be fully human comes late to Smiley. As a young man he is rather 'bloodless and inhuman' (*CD*, I, 12) and is attracted to spying initially because it allows him to make 'academic excursions into the mystery of human behaviour' (I, 10) and to work alone. However, the extreme solitude of operating under cover in Nazi Germany awakens Smiley to the need for emotional release, for something 'to take away the tension of his life' (I, 13). This need is satisfied by Ann, who teaches him to live intensely in and to grant reality to the present moment of experience: 'It was Ann who had ...

37

made the present so important and taught him the habit of reality' (V, 37–8).

Ann's profound influence on Smiley is evident in his affirmation, through a quotation from Goethe, that '*in the beginning was the deed*' (*HS*, VI, 128) and in his conviction that the only way to define what this deed should be is to do what 'you want to' (*TT*, X, 79). Furthermore, for Smiley, like Ann, 'intellectual or philosophical precepts' always break down in the face of 'the human situation' (*TT*, XXXVI, 322). However, Smiley goes beyond his teacher. Ann begins and ends in her feelings and each moment of experience constitutes an entirely new reality that need bear no relationship to what has gone before. As a result she is a complete solipsist. Smiley, on the other hand, escapes the trap of self-centredness by employing his rational or reflective faculty to make moral generalizations out of particular moments of experience. Thus, whereas both Smiley and Ann are 'unled', he is willing to accept the restraint of his 'own reason' (*SP*, XII, 136) and commits himself to an ideal of 'moderation' (*TT*, XXIII, 207), or what le Carré describes as 'his concept of a reasonable balance in human affairs' (*HS*, V, 118).

Although Smiley became a spy as a way of escaping the demands of feeling, his career in espionage turns out to be the one area of experience in which he comes close to achieving his goal of a balanced and complex humanity. As Ann's lover, Smiley is the helpless prey to his feelings, and as a scholar he encounters passion only as a literary convention. As a spy, on the other hand, he mediates brilliantly between the contradictory claims of the naive and the sentimental.

During his career at the Circus, Smiley disproves time and again the Sarratt doctrine that successful espionage is based entirely on technique, for his greatest triumphs come when he combines the demand for 'logical succession' (*SP*,

VIII, 86) with the guidance provided by his instincts, his feelings of concern for other people, and his acute awareness of the supremacy of the present moment and of facts over theory. As Peter Guillam puts it: 'If he ceases to care, he'll be half the operator he is' (*HS*, XIX, 461). This ability to combine feeling and reason is nowhere more evident than in Smiley's investigation into the murder of his former agent, Vladimir. Intense personal affection commits him to seek out Vladimir's murderers rather than conduct the cover-up for which he was commissioned. Instinct provides him with the vital first clue: 'Instinct – or better, a submerged perception yet to rise to the surface – signalled to him urgently that something about these cigarettes was wrong' (*SP*, VII, 77). And a logical and meticulous recreation of Vladimir's last moments enables him to uncover the missing cigarette packet that contains the information he needs (VIII, 84–7).

Even more revealing of Smiley's complex humanity is his willingness to face squarely and deal with the contradiction between ends and means inherent in British espionage. In Smiley's view spying is justified because it helps preserve a social system in which there is some scope for individualism, and hence for the cultivation of the naive aspect of the personality, from the threat posed by a communist enemy committed to the 'theory that the whole is more important than the individual' (*SC*, XII, 113). However, in pursuit of this goal the spy repeatedly commits acts of betrayal and treachery which constitute a total denial of the individual freedoms which he is supposedly defending. Smiley's task is, then, as he puts it himself, 'to be *inhuman in defence of our humanity* ... *harsh in defence of compassion*. To be *single-minded in defence of our disparity*' (*HS*, XIX, 461).

Throughout his career Smiley performs 'unprincipled act[s]' (*MQ*, IX, 218) and exploits the feelings of others. To ensure Ricki Tarr's continued cooperation he conceals from him the death of his beloved Irina; to extract information from Peter Worthington, he raises unjustified hopes of a reunion with a wife who has long since deserted him; to ensure the capture of Drake Ko, he blackmails the innocent bystander, Lizzie Worthington; and to force Karla's defection, he exploits his love for his daughter Tatiana.

Smiley's triumph is that he never seeks to evade the paradoxes inherent in his situation. Whereas characters like Control blunt their humanity and moral sense and those like Jim Prideaux engage in self-deception, Smiley accepts that, to remain human, he must continue to struggle painfully and inconclusively with the moral and emotional implications of his acts. His killing of the East German agent Dieter Frey is, for example, completely justified in terms of national security. Yet Smiley persists in mourning him as a man who was once his friend and accepts the guilty acknowledgment that, in holding back at a crucial moment in their death struggle, Dieter had 'remembered their friendship when Smiley had not', thereby proving himself the greater 'gentleman' (CD, XVI, 133). Similarly, Smiley can take no pleasure in the defeat of his life-long enemy, Karla, because he is acutely aware that as a consequence of the tactics he employed to reach his goal, he has been possessed by 'the very evil he had fought against' (SP, XXVII, 324).

In many ways the image of the suffering Smiley, which runs like a leitmotif through all the Smiley novels, and with which Smiley's People and hence the Smiley saga is brought to a conclusion, provides the key to le Carré's vision of the world. Given that this is the price of seeking full humanity in a world that is hostile to the feeling and loving aspects of the personality, it is not surprizing that so many of the characters are willing to seek refuge in self-deception and incompleteness. More significantly, though, from le Carré's perspective as a romantic, the fact that at least one man is willing to endure such pain serves as a glorious affirmation of the ability of the human urge for completeness to persist in the face of the most inhospitable circumstances.

CHAPTER TWO

# 'A World Grown Old and Cold and Weary': Description as Metaphor in le Carré's Novels

ACTION AND CHARACTER dominate John le Carré's novels. Passages of description are therefore relatively infrequent and usually brief. Nevertheless, their importance should not be underrated. Le Carré may be sparing in his evocations of building, place and landscape, but he is also remarkably consistent and purposeful, and in the course of his novels he creates a coherent and richly symbolic world which carries a major part of his thematic burden.[1] At the centre of this fictional world – as already suggested in the previous chapter – is Britain, a country with moribund tendencies which are powerfully expressed through images of darkness, decrepitude, emptiness and coldness. Description reveals the rest of Western Europe to be in much the same condition, although at times a cold, efficient sterility has replaced decay. In both cases descriptive passages are replete with a sense of loss or absence that points to the superiority of the past. Satisfactory alternatives to a Western Europe 'grown old and cold and weary'[2] are not easily found. American landscapes appear to be

---

[1] The technique of symbolic description plays an important part in le Carré's evocation of all the major countries in his novels, with the exception of Israel and Palestine in *The Little Drummer Girl*. His analysis of these societies and their relation to the rest of his fictional world is dealt with in ch. 5.

[2] This phrase is taken from lines by Rupert Brooke – 'To turn as swimmers into cleanness leaping/Glad from a world grown old and cold and weary' – which le

bright and spacious but are in reality meretricious, vulgar and militarist; Eastern European communist landscapes are even colder and darker than those of Western Europe and fail to make the faintest gesture towards something new.

East and West Europe and the United States are thus presented by le Carré as dark places. The source of darkness, he suggests implicitly throughout his novels and makes explicit in *The Naive and Sentimental Lover,* is to be found in a loss of fundamental human values. Consequently, only in his descriptions of Hong Kong – where despite the destructive influence of colonialism, Chinese culture retains values such as brotherly love and loyalty – does significant illumination enter le Carré's world. Le Carré is not, however, completely pessimistic about western society, and he demonstrates on a number of occasions how quickly the individual who acts in a human way can restore light to the world. In *The Naive and Sentimental Lover,* Shamus, who strives to live in accordance with the demands of his feelings, and who makes love his most important value, is consistently associated with light. Jim Prideaux in *Tinker, Tailor, Soldier, Spy* and Mr Cardew in *A Murder of Quality* are other characters whose intrinsic humanity brightens the landscapes in which they are located.

# I

Le Carré's descriptive techniques are most fully developed in his portrayal of Britain. Extensive detail plays a part in

Carré quotes in *The Looking-Glass War*, X, 105 and *Smiley's People*, XX, 252. The lines are taken from 'Peace', the first of Brooke's '1914' sonnets. See *The Collected Poems of Rupert Brooke* (New York: John Allen, 1915), p. 107.

the creation of only a few of his British scenes and, with the exception of some of the more purple passages of his early fiction, he does not draw attention to their larger significance. However, through careful repetition of a certain set of characteristics, he is able to create a complex and symbolically charged landscape. Three of le Carré's longer passages of description, drawn from novels written at different stages of his career, should establish the main outlines of his British landscape. The first appears in *The Looking-Glass War,* published in 1965, the second in *Tinker, Tailor, Soldier, Spy* (1974) and the third in *Smiley's People* (1980).

> The Department was housed in a crabbed, sooty villa of a place with a fire extinguisher on the balcony. It was like a house eternally for sale. No one knew why the Ministry put a wall round it; perhaps to protect it from the gaze of the people, like the wall round a cemetery; or the people from the gaze of the dead. Certainly not for the garden's sake, because nothing grew in it but grass which had worn away in patches like the coat of an old mongrel. The front door was painted dark green; it was never opened. By day anonymous vans of the same colour occasionally passed down the shabby drive, but they transacted their business in the back yard. . . . The building had that unmistakable air of controlled dilapidation which characterizes government hirings all over the world. For those who worked in it, its mystery was like the mystery of motherhood, its survival like the mystery of England. . . .
> Avery could remember it when the fog lingered contentedly against its stucco walls, or in the Summer, when the sunlight would briefly peer through the mesh curtains of his room, leaving no warmth, reveal-

ing no secrets. And he would remember it on that Winter dawn, its façade stained black, the street lights catching the raindrops on the grimy windows. (*LG*, II, 21–2)

The lobby [of the Circus] looked dingier than ever. Three old lifts, a wooden barrier, a poster for Mazawattee tea, Bryant's glass-fronted sentry box with a Scenes of England calendar and a line of mossy telephones. . . .
The grille of the centre lift rattled like a bunch of dry sticks. . . .
The net curtained window [of the duty officers' room] looked onto a courtyard full of blackened pipes. . . . In the daytime the place was used as a rest-room for girls with the vapours and to judge by the smell of cheap scent it still was. Along one wall lay the Rexine divan which at night made into a rotten bed; beside it the first-aid chest with the red cross peeling off the front, and a clapped-out television. . . .
When he opened the door [of the steel cupboard] dust rolled out of the bottom in a cloud, crawled a distance then slowly lifted towards the dark window. (*TT*, XI, 86, 91)

There are Victorian terraces in the region of Paddington Station that are painted as white as luxury liners on the outside, and inside are dark as tombs. Westbourne Terrace that Saturday morning gleamed as brightly as any of them, but the service road that led to Vladimir's part of it was blocked at one end by a heap of rotting mattresses, and by a smashed boom, like a frontier post, at the other. . . .
Shedding chestnut trees darkened the pillared doorway, a scarred cat eyed him warily. The doorbell was

45

the topmost of thirty but Smiley didn't press it
and when he shoved the double doors they swung
open too freely, revealing the same gloomy corridors
painted very shiny to defeat graffiti writers, and the
same linoleum staircase which squeaked like a hospital trolley. ... There was no light switch and the
stairs grew darker the higher he climbed. ... There
was a smell of too many people with not much money
jammed into too little air. (*SP*, VII, 71–2)

Britain, as presented in these and numerous similar
passages, is essentially urban and is filled with decaying ('rotting mattresses'; 'mossy telephones'), broken
('clapped-out television'; 'smashed boom') and disintegrating ('the first-aid chest with the red cross peeling off the
front'; 'the building had that unmistakable air of control-
led dilapidation') objects and buildings. It is almost always
dark ('dark window'; 'trees darkened the pillared doorway'; 'the stairs grew darker') and there is little colour.
Only the green door of the Department and the white
exterior of Westbourne Terrace relieve the uniform blackness of the scenes quoted above ('sooty villa'; 'façade
stained black'; 'blackened pipes'; 'gloomy corridors'). In
descriptions that appear elsewhere, black is often complemented by other minimal colours such as grey, white,
brown or a sickly yellow. Everything in Britain appears to
be dirty ('grimy windows'; 'the lobby looked dingier than
ever') and the air is filled with dust ('dust rolled out of the
bottom in a cloud'). Most of le Carré's descriptions are
characterized by a sense of confinement and even entrap-
ment ('a crabbed ... villa'; 'too many people ... jammed
into too little air'). And yet at the same time his scenes are
often empty or deserted. The Department, 'eternally for
sale', seems about to be abandoned, and in *Tinker, Tailor,
Soldier, Spy* Smiley visits a wine bar, 'with music playing

and no one there' (XI, 82) and a pub with 'the garden empty' (XVII, 149).

Recurring images of rot, dilapidation, dust, colourlessness and emptiness suggest that something is dead or dying. To reinforce this impression, le Carré frequently introduces imagery associated with death and disease. The wall around the Department is like 'a wall round a cemetery'; the inside of the Victorian terraces are 'dark as tombs'; and the staircase 'squeaked like a hospital trolley'. Similar metaphors are used throughout le Carré's work. The slate roof of the Sawley Arms is coloured 'the mauve of half mourning' (MQ, III, 172); 'the row of villas which lines Western Avenue is like a row of pink graves' (LG, VIII, 88); the music stands in Peter Worthington's room are 'crowded like skeletons into the corner of the room' (HS, X, 222).

Not even nature, on those rare occasions when it intrudes into le Carré's British landscape, offers any relief from the prevailing atmosphere of decay. Fog and rain are the prevailing weather conditions ('the fog lingered contentedly'; 'raindrops on the grimy windows') and when the sun does shine it leaves 'no warmth'. The grass in the Department garden is 'worn away in patches like the coat of an old mongrel' and the chestnut trees on Westbourne Terrace are 'shedding'. Scenes set in the country possess no more vitality. 'The rain rolled like gun-smoke down the brown combes of the Quantocks' (TT, I, 10) as Prideaux drives to Thursgood's and when Smiley walks on the beach near Marazion 'the day was grey, the seabirds were very white against the slate sea' (SP, XX, 252). Similarly, the beech trees on Hampstead Heath 'sank away from [Smiley] like a retreating army in the mist. The darkness had departed reluctantly, leaving an indoor gloom.' The little sunlight which leaks through is 'brown' and 'burned like a slow bonfire in its own smoke' (SP, VIII, 79–80).

47

By means of such descriptions le Carré creates a powerful and evocative, but obviously very selective landscape. Despite his reputation for working from photographs, le Carré's method is not photographic[3] and he deliberately excludes a great deal to create his desired effect. Places that show no sign of deterioration are, for example, almost never described. The hairdresser's in Curzon Street, from which Smiley sees Martindale emerge, is identified only by the name, Trumper's, because to do more would convey a visual message very different from le Carré's usual one. With its rich black marble and gold façade, its Royal crest and window display of old-fashioned, ivory-handled shaving equipment, Trumper's tells of an England still solid, wealthy and vigorously traditional.[4]

What guides le Carré in creating his British landscape is a desire, not so much to describe the place as it is – which is not to deny that what he does describe has an authentic ring – but to provide visual equivalents for its spiritual and moral condition. British society and culture as a whole have grown 'old and cold and weary' and are drawing close to, if they have not yet reached, death. This connection between landscape and the moribund state of the nation is made explicit by Peter Guillam's vision immediately prior to the unmasking of the mole Gerald: 'he saw the whole architecture of that night in apocalyptic terms: the signals on the railway bridge turned to gallows, the Victorian warehouses to gigantic prisons, their windows barred and arched against the misty sky. Closer at hand,

[3] Le Carré claims to have photographed all the locations used in *Tinker, Tailor, Soldier, Spy*. See 'John le Carré: Interviewed by Michael Dean', *Listener*, 92 (5 Sept. 1974), p. 307.
[4] George Trumper's is at 9 Curzon St. According to Henri Gault and Christian Millau, *The Best of London* (Los Angeles: The Knapp Press, 1982), p. 264, 'the interior has not changed since 1900 and in the midst of portraits of the Royal Family . . . and a collection of eighteenth-century wigs, you may purchase ivory-handled brushes'.

48

the ripple of rats and the stink of still water' (*TT*, XXXVI, 320).

The British landscape created by le Carré possesses a temporal as well as spatial dimension which enables him to express not only what Britain has become but also what has been lost. His descriptions thus remind us that the shoddy and disintegrating world of contemporary Britain is the last phase of a long and frequently impressive history that he traces back to pre-Roman times: 'The hills were olive and shaven, and had once been hill-forts' (*SP*, XX, 249). Le Carré achieves this historical perspective by focusing much of his description on places and buildings which, when they were created, embodied some of their society's major values and so now recall almost automatically their period of origin. The technique is firmly established in *A Murder of Quality*. King Arthur's Church, where, according to legend, Arthur paid homage to St Andrew, becomes an emblem of the post-Roman era when the dark age of myth gradually yielded to the light of Christianity. Carne Castle and Carne Abbey have similar symbolic implications: they stand for the joint aristocratic and ecclesiastical power upon which medieval society was founded. The ways in which aristocratic power endured and evolved from the Renaissance to the end of the eighteenth century, as domestic and political arts replaced military ones, are represented by the fortified manor house, Haverdown, in *the Naive and Sentimental Lover*, and the 'beautiful Palladian house' (XIII, 113), Millponds, in *Tinker, Tailor, Soldier, Spy*. It is, however, the Victorian and Edwardian eras that loom largest in le Carré's landscape. Carne, an ancient establishment, achieved full stature in this period. It stands as an emblem of the golden age of the public schools when, under the influence of Arnold's reforms at Rugby, they were largely responsible for producing a new type of morally earnest and Empire-minded ruling class. The great government buildings of London, most notably the Circus, recall the development of parliamentary democracy and the growth of a centralized bureaucracy. And the North Oxford house in *The Looking-Glass War,* with its 'pictures of some unknown family', its 'palm cross' and 'bible table' and its furniture 'of mahogany, with brass inlay' (XI, 125), is clearly a product of the Victorian bourgeois ideals of family, piety and solid materialism.

Enough is left of the original shape of these and other crumbling monuments to past greatness to provide the reader with a fairly precise picture of the values that are disappearing as Britain dies. What the architecture of the past suggests above all is that, at least up until the late nineteenth century, British society was infused with a sense of beauty, peace and order. The medieval Abbey Close at Carne is 'serene and beautiful' (*MQ*, III, 172) and the two clockwork knights who perform a courtly ritual to mark the half hours on the Abbey clock establish a close relationship between social and aesthetic order: 'the clock high above him struck the half-hour, and two knights on horseback rode out from their little castle over the door, and slowly raised their lances to each other in salute' (*MQ*, III, 172). Eighteenth-century buildings, such as the Georgian mansion in *Tinker, Tailor, Soldier, Spy,* possess similar qualities. The desire of the gambling club, which now occupies the premises, to lend an air of dignity to its proceedings makes this, ironically, one of the few well-preserved buildings in le Carré's novels and its original, elegant structure, based on contrasting circles and straight lines, is still very much in evidence: 'There were five steps and a brass doorbell in a scalloped recess. The door was black with pillars either side. ... He entered a circular hallway' (XXVI, 216). Connie describes the now ruined Millponds as being 'beautiful' with 'lovely grounds' (*TT,*

XIII, 113), and the drawing room of Smiley's house in Bywater Street is 'pretty' and 'tall, with eighteenth-century mouldings, long windows and a good fireplace' (SC, VI, 50).

The beauty and harmony of these buildings is usually complemented by a sense of spaciousness and solidity, the whole effect contrasting sharply with the ugly, fragmented, cramped and flimsy nature of the modern landscape. Thus, under its presumably recent covering of 'meagre coconut matting', the staircase at the Sawley Arms is 'wide' and made of 'marble' (MQ, IV, 187). The North Oxford house is also 'spacious' (LG, XI, 125) and its furniture is of mahogany and brass. Even more impressive in communicating a sense of space are Haverdown with its 'interminable' (NS, II, 27) corridors and 'forty acres' (I, 15) of grounds and the Victorian terraces near Paddington Station, the sweep and scope of which le Carré likens to 'luxury liners' (SP, VII, 71).

Also prominent in the historical periods to which le Carré alludes are objects and buildings created as expressions of the religious spirit. His novels include the early Christian King Arthur's Church, the medieval Carne Abbey, the bible desk in the Georgian mansion, the religious objects in the Victorian North Oxford house, and the possibly ancient but certainly pre-1920 parish church in Walliston (CD, III, 23). Their present condition clearly demonstrates that the spiritual impulse is part of what is dying in the modern world. King Arthur's Church is 'empty, falling to bits' (MQ, VII, 209); the Abbey saints are 'mutilated' (MQ, VI, 201); the bible desk holds the gambling club's membership book; and the parish church has been isolated by road development.

Just as le Carré's now disintegrating buildings were at one time graceful, harmonious and spacious, and were infused with a powerful spiritual quality, so there are signs that nature too was once a vital and life-enhancing force. Connie's photograph of Sarratt actually transports us into the past and, instead of the 'sorry place' encountered by Smiley in *Tinker, Tailor, Soldier, Spy*, where 'most of the elms had gone with the disease' and 'pylons burgeoned over the old cricket field' (XXXVII, 335), we see 'the grounds stretching out ... mown and sunlit and the sight screens glistening' (XIII, 111). The countryside around the Sercombe family home in Cornwall acquires a temporal dimension through a series of implied contrasts between its present sterility and past fruitfulness. References to 'a coppice of bare elms still waiting for the blight'; 'stubs of felled trees'; 'acres of smashed greenhouses'; 'an untended kitchen garden'; 'collapsed stables' (*SP*, XX, 249) contain powerful suggestions of a time when the trees thrived, the greenhouses and the garden nurtured growth, and horses occupied the stables. The existence of a gun room and a fishing room in the house further imply that the estate once supported wild as well as domestic animal life.

Modern buildings are relatively scarce in le Carré's British landscape and their nature as well as their number suggests the failure of attempts to revitalize the dying culture. These buildings fall into two categories: those which seek to revive past glories by imitating archaic styles and those which strive to express something new. The shoddiness, lack of imagination and spiritual poverty of modern Britain are equally evident in both. The first type not only domonstrate a lack of creative spirit but are also poor copies, substituting flimsy materials and mere decorative intentions for the solid and significant creations of the past. The medieval dungeon design of the Fleet Street 'ground-floor cellar' bar with its 'plastic prison arches' and 'fake muskets' (*TT*, XXVIII, 239) is typical in being both functionless and shoddy. Lacon's 'Berkshire Camelot' (*TT*, IV, 37) operates on a grander scale but is equally pointless.

'Stained-glass windows twenty feet high and a pine gallery over the entrance' seek to recreate the glories of a medieval manor but succeed only in making it 'the ugliest house for miles around' (*TT*, IV, 37). The Police Station at Carne, 'built ninety years ago to withstand the onslaughts of archery and battering rams' (*MQ*, III, 173), and the Fountain Café in suburban Walliston, 'all Tudor and horse brasses' (*CD*, IV, 31), are further examples of the futility of attempts to use the past to dignify the present.

The emptiness of the modern spirit is more directly evident in the second type of building, of which the tower block in St John's Wood is perhaps the best example. In front there is 'a large sculpture describing . . . nothing but a sort of cosmic muddle'. The use of 'terrazzo tile' and 'a banister of African teak' on the stairs which Smiley descends, demonstrates some concern with style and solidity, but it is one that lacks any hint of an authentic native voice. Further down even this is revealed to be a veneer aimed to cover the real cheapness and sordidness of the project: 'Rough-rendered plaster replaced the earlier luxury and a stench of uncollected refuse crammed the air' (*TT*, XXVII, 229). Other dimensions of the modern spirit are revealed by the motel room in which Smiley meets Jim Prideaux. Its matching yellow and orange fittings attempt to supply the vitality and good taste usually lacking in le Carré's British landscape, but in fact simply deprive everything in the room of individual identity. Even the label on the vodka bottle merges into the overall colour scheme. But what is more striking than the room's lack of individual character is its insubstantiality. Materials such as marble, mahogany and brass play no part in the construction of this place and 'the state of restlessness was constant. Even when the traffic outside went through one of its rare lulls the windows continued vibrating. In the bathroom the tooth glasses also vibrated, while from either wall and above them they could hear music, thumps and bits of conversation or laughter' (*TT*, XXXI, 263).

Le Carré's vision of a Britain caught between a decaying past and an empty, pointless present is epitomized by his description of the night of Haydon's capture. The Circus itself is not described, but it has been well established in earlier descriptions, such as the one quoted near the beginning of this chapter, as a rotting monument to the glory of British government institutions. Close to it are a number of shoddy buildings that strive for dignity by imitating aspects of the past: 'the buildings were gimcrack, cheaply fitted out with bits of empire: a Roman bank, a theatre like a vast desecrated mosque'. And in the background, advancing 'like an army of robots', are the 'high-rise blocks' (*TT*, XXXV, 314) which for le Carré are the most authentic expression of the absence from modern Britain of significant imaginative and spiritual qualities.


## II


Le Carré's Western European landscapes share many of the characteristics of his British ones. They are typically colourless, flat, dingy and incomplete and are usually shrouded in snow, rain or fog. As such they also communicate a sense of moral and spiritual *malaise,* an effect that le Carré again heightens by his use of death imagery. Finland, in *The Looking-Glass War,* is particularly corpse-like. Snow and mist cover everything and objects, 'drained of colour, black carrion on a white desert', possess 'no depth, no recession and no shadows' (I, 3). Figures and buildings are 'locked in the cold like bodies in an icefloe' (I, 3). Bonn is almost as bleak. The weather is persistently foggy and wet and its flat grey-white landscape is scarred with incomplete ('giant buildings, still unfinished' (*ST*, I, 6)) or fractured ('one hill . . . is broken like a quarry' (VII, 115)) objects. An atmosphere of death is pervasive. Farmhouses and new building estates look like 'hulks left over by the sea' (IV, 40) and the Bundestag is 'a vast motel mourned by its own flags' (XVII, 269).

Other German cities possess characteristics similar to Bonn's. As Leamas waits near the Berlin Wall he sees 'empty' (SC, I, 5) streets, and feels 'the icy October wind' (I, 7). The Wall itself is 'a dirty, ugly thing of breeze blocks and strands of barbed wire, lit with cheap yellow light' (I, 9). Smiley also experiences a 'half-world of ruin' (SC, I, 10) when, years later, he visits the Turkish quarter adjacent to the Wall to prepare for his final rendezvous with Karla. It is snowing and ferociously cold, and everything around him is either defunct ('the railway viaduct . . . was derelict, and no trains ever crossed'), decaying ('the shelter stank of leaf-mould and damp') or dead ('the warehouses . . . stood monstrous as the hulks of an earlier barbaric civilisation (SP, XXVII, 323)). The Olympic Village in Munich, although the product of a much more hopeful spirit, is in no better condition than the Berlin Wall: 'The Village is not a village at all, of course, but a marooned and disintegrating citadel of grey concrete' (LD, II, 32). The staircase leading up to Kurtz's apartment there is 'filthy' (II, 32) and the apartment itself 'awfully down-at-heel' with windows that offer a 'grimy view of the road to Dachau' (II, 33). The other Munich apartment occupied by the Israelis is 'pervaded with an air of sad neglect' which creates 'a mood of bereavement' (II, 34).

Le Carré's German landscapes often possess an historical dimension which suggests as clearly as do the British the superiority of the past. Repeated reminders that the hills around Bonn were 'the land of the Nibelungs' and that the Drachenfels is 'where Siegfried had slain the dragon and bathed in its magic blood' (ST, VII, 108) serve, for example, to establish a sharp contrast between the courage, purposefulness and vitality of the German heroic age, and the aimless time-serving that characterizes modern Bonn. However, this division between past and present, le Carré suggests in his descriptions of Dresden and Hamburg, is even more marked than in Britain because of the wholesale destruction and rebuilding which resulted from war-time bombing. Pre-war Dresden is emblematic of much of what was best in the German past: Smiley 'had loved its architecture, its odd jumble of medieval and classical buildings, sometimes reminiscent of Oxford, its cupolas, towers and spires, its copper-green roofs shimmering under a hot sun' (CD, XIV, 110). The Second World War not only obliterates all this but, by stranding Dresden in the eastern part of a divided Germany, commits its future to a communist ideology that is completely alien to the spirit of individuality, creativity and spirituality so powerfully present in its past. Even though it remains in the West, the contrast between the pre- and post-war cities of Hamburg is almost as great. Reduced by war to 'one endless smouldering bomb-site', Hamburg has been reborn as a place 'hurtling into the anonymity of canned music, high-rise concrete and smoked glass' (SP, XVI, 184). Thus, the 'ancient, free, and Hanseatic City' (II, 27) which Smiley remembers from his youth as 'a rich and graceful shipping town' (XVI, 184) is 'now almost pounded to death by the thunder of its own prosperity' (II, 27).

The differences between contemporary Europe, particularly Germany, with its expensive but sterile landscapes created by the post-war rebuilding process and Britain, with its rotting remnants of former greatness, are epitomized by two descriptions of places dedicated to the sale of sex. The Pussywillow Club in Soho which Leamas visits in *The Spy Who Came in from the Cold* is located down 'a narrow alley, at the far end of which shone a tawdry neon sign' (VII, 60). Music is provided by a 'two-piece band' which produces a 'subdued moan' (VII, 60–1), and the stripper is 'a young, drab girl with a dark bruise on her thigh. She had that pitiful, spindly nakedness which is embarrassing because it is not erotic' (VII, 61). The Blue Diamond Club in Hamburg is also to be found in an alley, but otherwise is very different. The anteroom is 'trim' and 'filled with grey machinery manned by a smart young man in a grey suit'. On the desk there is 'an elaborate telephone system' (*SP*, XVI, 185). Doors open electronically to reveal girls who are 'beautiful, naked and young' (XVI, 187). The manager's office is 'clean as a doctor's surgery with a polished plastic desk and a lot more machinery' (XVI, 188).

No healthy human impulse or real vitality is to be found in either place. The Soho stripper is not erotic and Smiley finds the 'demonstration of love-making' staged at the Blue Diamond 'mechanical, pointless, dispiriting' (XVI, 187). However, the British setting does at least hint at some former energy now drained away. Feeble though it may be, the music is still produced by people, thereby connecting it, if only remotely, to one of the most significant of the human creative acts. Similarly, the stripper may be bruised, but this at least affirms that she is flesh and blood and distantly related to an ideal of whole and fecund female beauty and sexuality. The Blue Diamond, on the other hand, with its emphasis on efficiency, technology and profit, is completely divorced from the finer human urges and bears no relationship whatsoever to the spirit that lies behind the myths of the *Nibelungen* or the old city of Dresden.

As was the case with British architecture such as the St John's Wood tower block, but on a much larger scale, European efforts to create something new thus reveal nothing more than the poverty of the modern spirit. That there is some recognition of this is made evident by occasional attempts to shape contemporary buildings along traditional lines. However, as with similar efforts in Britain, these anachronistic creations fail completely to recapture any of the glories of the past and serve only to reinforce our sense of the inferiority of the present. This is true, for instance, of the motel outside Munich which 'had been built twelve months ago for medievally-minded lovers, with cement-stippled cloisters, plastic muskets, and tinted neon lighting' (*LD*, XV, 247).

Le Carré makes his point most tellingly by juxtaposing descriptions of the Bellevue Palace Hotel in Berne and the café-restaurant in Thun. The former is a rare example of something old that retains its original grandeur. It is 'an enormous, sumptuous place of mellowed Edwardian quiet' (*SP*, XX, 254) and Smiley's room is 'a tiny Swiss Versailles. The *bombé* writing-desk had brass inlay and a marble top, a Bartlett print of Lord Byron's Childe Harold hung above the pristine twin beds' (XXI, 255). The café, which le Carré describes as 'modern Swiss antique' (XXIII, 266), offers nothing more than a pathetic parody of the values the hotel represents. Where the Bellevue Palace employs materials that demonstrate a concern for beauty and durability, the café has 'stucco pillars' on which hang 'plastic lances' (XXIII, 266). Similarly, the integration of function and form evident in the writing desk with its brass inlay and marble top has been replaced by the merely decorative: 'The lamps were wrought iron but the illumination came from a ring of strip lighting round the ceiling' (XXIII, 266). Finally, the values of generosity and hospitality suggested by the adjectives 'enormous', 'sumptuous' and 'mellowed' have diminished into the stingy and grudging attitude epitomized by the waitress who denies Smiley's request that his *café-crème* be served in a glass.

Through description, then, le Carré offers us a vision of

the decline of the major Western European nations. Images of social harmony, aesthetic wholeness and cultural and spiritual vitality all belong to the past and the modern world is characterized either by decay or by sterile and mechanical innovation. However, if we broaden le Carré's canvas to include communist-bloc and American landscapes we can see that he finds little that is appealing in the alternatives that lie to the East or to the West.

## III

None of le Carré's novels is set in the United States, but a number of scenes take place in American Embassies and military bases and these provide the basis for the creation of a sketchily defined but evocative landscape. At first sight, this American landscape with its *'dimension'*, 'optimism' (*ST*, VII, 109) and dazzling illumination ('the American Embassy, brilliant as a power house, drove yellow shafts through the mist' (XI, 180)) offers an attractive alternative to the constricted and dark vistas of Western Europe. There is, for example, a marked contrast between the entertainment facilities of British and American intelligence. Whereas the British provide hospitality in a gutted Circus, serving drinks from 'a trestle table' with 'a darned damask tablecloth spread over it', the Americans have a 'vast rooftop bar, known within the Circus as the planetarium' (*HS*, XII, 262), which provides superb views across London. However, the sense of vision proves to be false, the brilliance illusory and the optimism ill-founded. Martello's office is impressive because of its size, but it is finally more significant that the rosewood table is 'fake',[5]

---

[5] The adjective 'fake' is added to the text in the Knopf edition of the novel. See *The Honourable Schoolboy* (Knopf edition), p. 256.

and that the room is furnished with 'airline chairs' and an 'empty' (XII, 263) desk. As these images suggest, the Americans lack any authentic vision or sense of personal identity with which to fill their territory. All they have to offer is a shallow patriotism symbolized by the flag and the Presidential portraits to be found in both Martello's office and the American Embassy in Hong Kong. As a result the feeling of spaciousness is quickly transformed into one of arid bareness.

In a sense, le Carré's Americans are a pathetic people whose brilliance reveals nothing but their own emptiness. However, he has little pity to spare for them because out of their unthinking patriotism springs the conviction that it is justifiable to use arms to propagate the American way of life.[6] During Westerby's swing through the Asian war zone, we are given repeated glimpses of the disastrous consequences of the Americans' stupid assumption that they have a right to impose a set of values characterized by a jumble of messages about 'higher education', 'cut-price washing machines' and 'prayer' (XVIII, 438) on other cultures. Enclosed behind 'smoked glass' windows, in 'soundproof' (XVIII, 437) rooms which, with their 'fake fireplace[s]' and 'Andrew Wyeth reproduction[s]' (XVIII, 435), fail to make any concession to the local environment, the American military is completely unequipped to recognize that 'electronics base[s]' (XVIII, 446) dumped in the midst of paddie fields are inadequate compensation for the

---

[6] Le Carré has suggested that literary considerations alone are responsible for his generally negative presentation of the Americans. His argument is that, in order to put the weight of his stories on the British, the Americans must be made unpopular and hence removed from the picture. However, the scorn expressed for the Americans in *The Honourable Schoolboy* is so intense as to suggest a source in personal antipathy rather than literary necessity. For le Carré's comments on the role played by the United States in his novels see Andrew Rutherford, 'Spymaster', *Kaleidoscope*, BBC Radio 4, 13 Sept. 1979 (transcript, p. 10).

destruction of a vibrant and at times magical culture: 'From the river thirty feet below them came the murmured chant of the sampans as they drifted like long leaves across the golden moon-path. From the sky ... came the occasional ragged flashes of outgoing gunfire' (XVI, 384). For le Carré, a society which is willing to replace this 'golden moon-path' with 'a single infernal light, like the promise of a future war' (XVIII, 446) has little to offer as an alternative even to the most decadent of the older democracies. In the final analysis, the light the Americans emit not only exposes their hollowness, it also blinds the viewer to their ugliness. At night the American aircraft carrier makes a brave show in Hong Kong harbour, where 'floodlit and dressed overall, [it] basked like a pampered woman amid a cluster of attendant launches' (XX, 476). Viewed in daylight it proves to be 'grey and menacing, like an unsheathed knife' (XXI, 505). Similarly the lights that suddenly brighten the sky above Po Toi during the festival of Tin Hau, prove not to be a means of revealing the godhead but of 'blinding' those below to the presence of 'blackened [American] helicopters' (XXI, 523) on a mission of slaughter.

Communist Europe is, however, even less appealing than the United States, and le Carré's descriptions of East Germany are the ugliest, bleakest and most despairing of any that appear in his novels. To some extent East Germany simply shares the *malaise* from which Britain and Western Europe suffer. Its landscapes, both urban and rural, are characterized by the same lack of colour, the same darkness, emptiness, sense of disintegration and decay, and continual rain as those to the West. The Church tower in Kalkstadt is 'black and empty' (*LG*, XIX, 214); Leiser's room in the town is 'large and bare', with walls of 'grey plaster' over which 'the damp had spread ... in dark shadows' (XX, 215). The street lights close to the Berlin

Wall are 'dingy' (*SC*, XXV, 216), the market stalls 'empty'. A fence is 'broken' and a building 'windowless' (XXV, 217). Empty doorways 'gaped sightlessly' and the Wall itself is 'grey-brown in the weary arclight' (XXV, 218). Alec Leamas passes through this despairing scene in the rain and 'pitch dark' (XXV, 218). The Peace Hall in Leipzig is made of 'pre-cast concrete with ... cracks in the corners' and is decorated with 'dusty' bunting which 'looked like something from a fascist funeral' (*SC*, XIX, 161). Rural scenes are no less drab and sterile: 'The steep wooded hills on either side gradually yielded their colours to the gathering dusk until they stood grey and lifeless in the twilight' (XIV, 136).

Significant colour appears only once in all of le Carré's Eastern European scenes. In the secret courtroom where Leamas is exposed as a double agent, red stands out in sharp contrast to the otherwise unremitting shades of black and grey: 'Above them, suspended from the ceiling by three loops of wire, was a large red star made of plywood' (*SC*, XX, 164). However, since the star is the symbol of the communist absolutism responsible for the bleak and colourless landscape over which it presides, the use of colour here is clearly ironic. Light is employed towards similarly ironic ends on the one occasion that it penetrates the all-pervading gloom. As is the case with the American helicopter in *The Honourable Schoolboy*, the searchlights that play on the Berlin Wall during Leamas's attempt to escape blind rather than illuminate and are harbingers of death rather than revelation:

Suddenly the whole world seemed to break into flame; from everywhere, from above and beside them, massive lights converged, bursting upon them with savage accuracy.
Leamas was blinded. ... He could see nothing –

only a mad confusion of colour dancing in his eyes.
Shielding his eyes he looked down at the foot of the wall and at last he managed to see her, lying still. . . . She was dead.
Finally they shot him, two or three shots. He stood glaring round him like a blinded bull in the arena. (*SC*, XXVI, 221–2)

Eastern Europe is, finally, the most desolate of all le Carré's landscapes because it does not contain even the hint of a desire to find something new with which to replace the crumbling fragments of a defunct culture. As Leiser travels across East Germany he observes all around him decay and destruction: 'The house was old, falling with neglect; the drive overgrown with grass, pitted with cart tracks. The fences were broken' (*LG*, XVIII, 205). But what strikes him most is the complete lack of interest in doing anything to halt the process of disintegration: 'There were no signposts and no new buildings, it suddenly occurred to him. That was where the peace came from, it was the peace of no innovation – it might have been fifty years ago, a hundred. . . . It was the darkness of indifference' (XVIII, 203–4). The spirit of 'innovation' responsible for the terrazzo tile and African teak banisters in the St John's Wood tower block does not lead to happy results. Nevertheless, it does demonstrate that in Britain the will to make things new still exists, if only feebly. By contrast there is such a profound indifference in East Germany that anything new which is built, such as the block of workers' flats in Kalkstadt, is simply designed to conform to the prevailing grey drabness. Everything about these flats, from their 'shoddy walls' (*LG*, XXIII, 242) and location on 'a patch of waste land' (XXI, 228), to the failure to give them a name, demonstrates a total lack of the creative impulse. Consequently, the atmosphere which emanates from the place is one that we would associate usually with something close to death rather than newly born: 'Pale lights shone in almost every window; six floors. Stone steps, thick with leaves, led to the cellar. . . . The first room was large and airless' (XXIII, 242).

## IV

Le Carré's landscapes define the modern world as a dark place, lacking moral or spiritual illumination. However, if we explore this use of dark and light as an aspect of description a little further, we can see that le Carré's pessimism is not absolute, and that he is willing to suggest ways in which the death of modern civilization can be prevented. Such a study must take as its starting point an examination of the role of Hong Kong in the novelist's world landscape.

To a certain extent le Carré employs Hong Kong in *The Honourable Schoolboy* as a part of his analysis of the decline of British society, for even as it is sinking into its own deathbed, Britain has reached out a palsied arm and presumed to infect another culture with its disease. Displaying insensitivity to the authenticity of other ways of life almost equal to that of the Americans in Vietnam and Cambodia, the British colonialists have imposed on Hong Kong a network of their own sterile customs. The tedious rituals of the Foreign Correspondents' Club, the dull cricket games played by the 'Peak mafia' (*HS*, VI, 127), and race-track presentations modelled on prize-giving ceremonies at English village fêtes (VII, 165–6) make Hong Kong society seem almost as lifeless as that in Britain. Even worse the mixture of incompatible cultures which results from the British presence often has ludicrous results, as, for example, in 'the Tudor pub in the unfinished high-rise building' and the 'rooftop bar ... with its four-piece Chinese band playing Noël Coward, and its straight-faced Chinese barmen in periwigs and frock-coats' (IX, 211).

However, Hong Kong functions as more than a symbol of the destructive effects of colonialism, for it also possesses a vitality, energy, beauty and quality of illumination rarely found in le Carré's novels. The following descriptions are typical: 'Behind the black Peak a full moon, not yet risen, glowed like a forest fire' (XIII, 291); 'the harbour lay like a perfect mirror at the centre of the jewel box' (XIII, 293); 'Behind him hung the Peak, its shoulders festooned in gold lights' (XX, 476). The source of this beauty and light is to be found in the ability of the Chinese, at some fundamental level, to resist the taint of British influence. Westerby is acutely conscious that in essentials, Chinese society is completely hidden from the 'roundeye' who 'could live all his life in the same block and never have the smallest notion of the secret tic-tac on his doorstep' (IV, 125–6). After twenty-five years in the East, he finds it as 'obscure' (VI, 126) as ever. Thus, when the Chinese go about their own business they do so in a spirit very different from the British, and there is a sharp contrast, for instance, between life on the roof-tops and on the cricket field. Whereas the one is 'a breathtaking theatre of survival' embodying sweat-shops, religious services, mah-jong games, fortune telling and schools for 'dancing, reading, ballet, recreation and combat' (VI, 123), the other involves 'fifteen whiteclad figures' who 'lounged' 'on a patch of perfect English lawn', at the beginning of 'a long dull innings to no applause' (IV, 127).

The Chinese direct their energy, as the roof-top scene suggests, towards a rich variety of objects, ranging from the grossly materialistic to the deeply spiritual. However, for le Carré, the society's vitality is rooted in the ability of its members to remain committed to some fundamental human concerns of which the British have, by and large, lost sight. Drake Ko, le Carré's only fully developed Chinese character, is an entrepreneur and a quasi-gangster, who will kill if crossed. Yet his behaviour is rooted in a consistent moral system that demands complete loyalty to family, clan and those with whom he has created a bond of trust. For Ko, one must 'hold fast to that which is good. . . . That is what God likes' (XXI, 512) and the chance of reunion with a brother whom he 'loved' (XXI, 513) justifies risking everything. Thus, Lizzie Worthington, the only British character who comes close to understanding Ko, is anxious, above all, to convince him that, 'I kept faith. . . . I stuck to the deal' because 'it's what he cares about most' (XXI, 515).

There is, therefore, a direct relationship between the presence of light in le Carré's Hong Kong landscape and the society's ability to retain contact with those basic human urges defined in chapter 1. How western societies are to follow the example set by Hong Kong and escape their prevailing darkness is a problem to which le Carré provides no ready answers. However, through a number of scenes in which landscape is related to character rather than country, he does suggest that the beginnings of a solution lie within the power of each of us; by maintaining or regaining contact with the instinctual bases of personality any individual can restore some value or light to the world. Carne, one of the most sterile places in all of le Carré's novels, is, for example, briefly transformed under the influence of Mr Cardew, a man of spiritual insight and personal warmth. His Tabernacle is not cheap, crumbling or dirty but is a place of 'thickly-varnished ochre pine' and an active 'polishing' of 'the heavy brass chandelier'. To one side, there is 'a small vegetable garden, carefully tilled, with bright yellow paths running between the empty beds'. Mr Cardew has created an oasis within the modern desert and it is apt that on the day Smiley visits him, instead of the usual rain and gloom, 'the sun shone through the crisp air. It was a cold, beautiful day' (*MQ*, XII, 243).

A similar relationship is established between landscape and character during the episode when Smiley questions Jim Prideaux. For all his limitations, Prideaux is fundamentally a good human being motivated by love for his fellow men and for his country. These qualities shine through his account of the otherwise sordid Operation Testify. As Jim's story gets under way and his naive vision begins to make itself felt, it is appropriate that he and Smiley move out of the confined, cheap and restless motel and to 'a hilltop free of fog'. Here a 'long view' is possible, 'scattered lights reached into the distance', 'the sky was light' (*TT*, XXI, 265), and 'the stars were very clear' (XXXI, 270). In contrast to the night of Operation Testify when there was 'no moon' (XXXI, 275), on this occasion 'the half moon was free of cloud' (XXXI, 274). Under Prideaux's influence the landscape is, albeit only temporarily, transformed: 'The night landscape seemed to Smiley suddenly innocent; it was like a great canvas on which nothing bad or cruel had ever been painted' (XXXII, 287–8).

This ability of the individual to reintroduce light into the world is explored most fully and most explicitly in *The Naive and Sentimental Lover*. Shamus's determination to live in accordance with the dictates of his feelings and to pursue the ideal of love is defined quite specifically as a search for light and a rejection of darkness: 'We don't want *all right*, do we, lover. . . . Never did, never will. We want the sun, not the fucking twilight' (XXIV, 252). Similarly, Helen comments that Shamus is fighting 'greyness' (XXVII, 281) and defines Cassidy's final failure to put a value on himself, as going 'back into that awful dark' (XXXVIII, 410, 411).

The effect that an individual such as Shamus can have on a dying culture becomes evident during Cassidy's visit to Haverdown. Haverdown itself is one of le Carré's clearest symbols of the decline of Britain. Begun in the thirteenth century its architecture reflects the main stages in English history up the Georgian period. Today, however, it is neglected and in decay, a process le Carré emphasizes through ironic contrasts between the estate agent's idealized description of the place and the modern actuality: '*The entrance is marked by a Pair of finely pointed stone gateposts surmounted by ornamental Beasts dating from the sixteenth Century.* Directly before him, two disintegrating griffins, glumly clutching armorial shields, rose into the green darkness of a beech tree' (I, 14). What Cassidy sees as he views Haverdown in 'twilight' is 'the hulk of a dozen English generations', and just as the light is 'dying' (I, 19), so, it seems, is Britain.

However, the elegiac tone which has pervaded the scene up to this point is broken when 'a real light' (I, 20) suddenly penetrates the gloom, announcing the arrival of Shamus. At first Shamus's features are hidden by the glow of the lamp and so for Cassidy, Shamus's identity is entirely bound up in the light. When Shamus answers a question, it seems to Cassidy that 'the lantern replied' (II, 22). This identification of Shamus with light is further intensified by the way in which his face is eventually revealed to Cassidy: 'In the same moment a ray of red sunlight, reflected from the upper window of the chapel, broke like a tiny dawn over the interior of the porch and provided Cassidy with a first sight of his examiner' (II, 23). From here on until the souring of their relationship as a consequence of Cassidy's affair with Helen, Shamus consistently brightens the gloomy modern world for Cassidy. Cassidy's experience of 'standing in the total blackness of an unknown interior with only his host's friendly grasp to guide him' reminds him of waiting in the cinema for the 'grey rectangle' (II, 25) to be drawn back and the brilliantly lit screen to be revealed. However, whereas cinematic light produces only 'hallucinations' (II, 25), Shamus offers genuine enlightenment.

Shamus assumes his role as Cassidy's guide during this first evening. By keeping control of the lantern while showing Cassidy over the house, he is the source of what little illumination is possible in this dark and dying place. At the end of the tour his lantern, assisted by the firelight, provides Cassidy with his first view of Helen. So 'utterly improbable' is this fleeting vision of naked beauty that Cassidy might have dismissed it as an illusion 'had not the beam of the lantern firmly pointed him the proof of her terrestial existence' (II, 31). As Shamus's influence grows, so it seems the world responds by becoming lighter: 'shoulder to shoulder' during their 'pee-break', Shamus and Cassidy view the night in its 'alpine majesty' and see the house rise 'in countless peaks against the pale sky, where powdery swarms of stars followed the moonlit ridges of the clouds like fireflies frozen into the external ice. At their feet a white dew glistened' (IV, 43). It is, as Shamus comments, quoting Joyce, 'the heaventree of stars. ... Hung with humid nightree fruit' (IV, 43), that Cassidy is seeing for the first time. Later in the evening Shamus takes Cassidy to a pub 'higher up the hill . . . a leafy place with a verandah and a long view of the valley lights. The lights reached to the edge of the earth, melting together in a low haze of gold before joining the descending stars' (VI, 62–3). The night light is equally magical during Shamus and Cassidy's 'love affair' (XVI, 161) in Paris: 'Diamonds surrounded them: hung in giant clusters in the window panes, pricked the orange night sky, were draped in the eyes of lovers and in the brown silk of women's hair' (XVII, 177). On the first day of this same trip, Cassidy experiences the even more brilliant illumination of the sun: Paris is 'bathed in perfect sunlight. It fired the river, shimmered in the pink streets, and turned the golden eagles into phoenixes of present joy' (XVI, 162–3).

The light created by Cassidy and Shamus's relationship, in which for a while 'one perfect summer's day followed another' (XXV, 267), eventually fades and, in the climactic alpine scenes, the landscape emanates once again an atmosphere of death. Indeed, the snow that falls and covers everything as Cassidy betrays his commitment to Helen comes close to suggesting, as it does in the similar scene with which Joyce ends 'The Dead', the inevitable annihilation of all life:

> The snow had almost covered them. Sometimes he saw them, sometimes there was nothing; it was no longer possible to tell. Once, through a clearing as it were, he made out two uprights, one straight and one crooked, and either they were posts along the fencing or two people leaning together as they struggled with the very deep snow. But . . . they vanished finally, into the nothing that lay beyond the blizzard. (XXXVII, 411)

Like Prideaux, Shamus is therefore unable to make the world innocent for very long; the efforts of both men are nonetheless significant, for they demonstrate that redemption is possible. Given the dreadful bleakness of landscapes stripped of the force of love, it seems inevitable that there will be other occasions upon which the naive spirit will assert itself.

A study of le Carré's landscapes leaves the reader face to face once again with the paradoxes that lie at the centre of his vision. As a social critic he presents powerful metaphors for a world that has lost its vital spark and is dying, and nothing the individual can do seems likely to reverse this process. And yet, as a romantic, le Carré attaches great significance to any life-affirming gesture, and is ever ready to celebrate those occasions, however fleeting, on which one of his characters is able to infuse a dreary landscape with glorious light.

# CHAPTER THREE

# Le Carré and the Spy Novel

ARLIER CHAPTERS HAVE revealed John le Carré to be a serious artist capable of embodying complex themes within a significant literary framework. The espionage world plays an important part in his total achievement because it provides a useful vantage point from which to view a number of issues inherent in the conflict between the naive and sentimental aspects of the self and because it is a subculture which reflects some of the major tendencies in contemporary British society. Some even more fundamental questions about the role of spying in le Carré's fiction still remain to be asked, for le Carré is not simply a writer who makes some use of espionage subject matter. On the contrary, he constructs his novels, with the exception of *The Naive and Sentimental Lover* and *A Murder of Quality*, almost entirely out of the formulas of spy fiction. Consequently, any claims that might be made about le Carré's achievement must be based firmly on an understanding of his place within the tradition of the spy novel and of the ways in which he makes its character types, conventions and patterns of action serve his own artistic ends.

There are numerous allusions scattered throughout le Carré's novels which warn the reader not only that his roots are to be found in espionage fiction, as much as in the great literature of the English and European traditions, but also that le Carré is thoroughly imbued in the work of all types of spy novelists, ranging from simple entertainers to writers who have anticipated him in seeking out the genre's artistic potential. The epigraphs to the four sections of *The Looking-Glass War* make the status le Carré wishes to grant the spy novel particularly obvious, for he sets off quotations from Kipling's *Kim* and Buchan's *Mr Standfast* against lines from W. H. Auden and Rupert Brooke. Elsewhere in his novels further allusions to popular writers of espionage fiction are introduced to balance frequent references to Joseph Conrad and Graham Greene. Both contribute, for example, to the names and situations of Jerry Westerby and Jim Prideaux.

Westerby is probably modelled in part on Conrad's Axel Heyst, as L. R. Leavis and J. M. Blom suggest,[1] and his attitude to American imperialism in Vietnam and Cambodia closely resembles that of Fowler in Greene's *The Quiet American*. At the same time, though, his discovery and loss of love in Tuscany clearly recalls Hugh Morrice's similar experience in the same place in William Le Queux's *Revelations of the Secret Service*.[2] Jim Prideaux too has origins in Conrad since he shares more than a Christian name with the hero of *Lord Jim*. Both are idealistic dreamers who have read too much heroic schoolboy literature, and both find a kind of salvation in special worlds – Thursgood's School and Patusan – that accord with the logic of their imagination rather than the facts of everyday reality. But Jim's nickname, Rhino, and his preference for the novels of John Buchan (*TT*, XXX, 262) suggest that Bulldog Drummond's athleticism, public school ethics and lack of introspection, and Richard Hannay's fundamental decency and simple military stoicism were

---

[1] L. R. Leavis and J. M. Blom, 'Current Literature, 1977', *English Studies*, 59 (1978), p. 447.
[2] (London: F. V. White, 1911), pp. 5–20.

equally influential in shaping his character.

The double pattern of allusion evident in these examples continues throughout le Carré's novels. Conrad's secret sharer motif is echoed on a number of occasions,[3] most explicitly in *Smiley's People*: Smiley 'began plodding through the long galleries of his professional memory ... looking for the one hallowed face that, like a secret sharer, seemed to have swum out of the little contact photograph to board his faltering consciousness' (XII, 132). An equally obvious reference to Conrad is contained within Lizzie Worthington's use, in *The Honourable Schoolboy,* of the famous phrase 'one of us' (XXI, 496), which reverberates throughout *Lord Jim.*[4] The most pointed of all le Carré's allusions to Conrad, however, is to be found in *The Little Drummer Girl,* where the heroine, Charlie, and Kurtz and Joseph, the Israeli agents who handle her, are named after the two main characters and the author of *Heart of Darkness.*[5] Graham Greene is most clearly present in *Tinker, Tailor, Soldier, Spy,* for when Prideaux tells his schoolboy helper, Roach, that he is the 'best watcher in the unit' (I, 16) he reminds the reader of that other agent-child relationship in *The Confidential Agent* and, in particular, of D.'s description of Else as 'a good watcher'.[6]

Of le Carré's many allusions to popular spy novels the following should suffice as examples. In *Tinker, Tailor, Soldier, Spy* Bill Haydon describes spying as 'The Great

---

[3] See James Wolcott's discussion of this topic, 'The Secret Sharers', *New York Review of Books,* 14 April 1983, p. 19.

[4] See for example *Lord Jim* (Edinburgh: John Grant, 1925), p. 416.

[5] Wolcott, p. 19 points out the Conradian allusions contained within the names Kurtz and Joseph but, oddly enough, makes no comment on Charlie.

[6] Graham Greene, *The Confidential Agent* (London: Heinemann, 1939), p. 60. All subsequent references to the works of Graham Greene will be cited in the text. The other editions used are *The Quiet American* (London: Heinemann and Bodley Head, 1955); *Our Man in Havana* (London: Heinemann and Bodley Head, 1958); *The Human Factor* (London: Heinemann and Bodley Head, 1978).

Game' (XXXIX, 250), thereby recalling Rudyard Kipling's *Kim*,[7] and in *The Honourable Schoolboy*, Enderby notes that questions of Chinese thumb prints seem more appropriate to the novels of Oppenheim than to the realities of contemporary espionage (VIII, 179). *The Honourable Schoolboy* is also the source of two references to Ian Fleming's *You Only Live Twice*. First, Guillam's whimsical plan to start a chicken farm where he will live in bucolic isolation with Molly Meakin should he be expelled from the Circus (VIII, 193), reiterates James Bond's thoughts as he anticipates the end of his career as an agent: 'It's always exciting starting a new life. Anyway, who's afraid of the Big Bad M? Will you [Mary Goodnight] come and lend a hand on my chicken farm?'[8] Second, le Carré's Craw is connected to Fleming's Dikko Henderson through a common source in the Australian journalist, Richard Hughes.[9]

Despite the clues provided by this pattern of allusion, le Carré's critics have not always been willing to go far enough in seeking his place within the tradition of the spy novel. To argue, as John Halperin does,[10] that le Carré deglamourizes spying and belongs exclusively to the Conrad-Greene school of realistic espionage fiction, is to place too much emphasis on his cynical attitude to modern espionage and on his jaundiced view of British

[7] Rudyard Kipling, *Kim* (London: Macmillan, 1961), p. 162.

[8] Ian Fleming, *You Only Live Twice* (London: Triad/Granada, 1978), p. 27.

[9] Le Carré claims that it was not until he wrote to Richard Hughes for permission to include him in *The Honourable Schoolboy* that he learnt of his earlier fictional appearance in *You Only Live Twice*. However, he has admitted on a number of occasions that he is familiar with the James Bond novels. For the comment about Richard Hughes see 'John le Carré: An Interrogation', interview with Michael Barber, *New York Times Book Review*, 25 Sept. 1977, p. 45. For evidence of le Carré's familiarity with Bond, see his television interview with Malcolm Muggeridge, *Intimations*, BBC 2, 8 Feb. 1966, transcript, p. 6.

[10] 'Between Two Worlds', *South Atlantic Quarterly*, 79 (Winter 1980), pp. 17, 18–19.

society, at the expense of the deep vein of romanticism which runs through his novels and to which they owe much of their complexity. A proper understanding of le Carré's achievement as a spy novelist must be based on his ability – as revealed, for instance, in his complex portraits of Jim Prideaux and Jerry Westerby, Buchan heroes who have strayed into the modern world – to satirize the simplistic values and easy optimism of the traditional spy novel and yet at the same time to persuade the reader that there is something to admire in it. As T. J. Binyon points out in his review of *The Honourable Schoolboy*, le Carré 'assimilates – if ironically – rather than rejects the former tradition of the spy novel'[11] and it will be the task of this chapter to explore the terms under which the assimilation takes place.

It is essential to arrive at a rather more precise definition of le Carré's relationship to Conrad and Greene than that offered by critics like Halperin. Certainly, the influence of Conrad and Greene is a profound one and both have taught le Carré a good deal about the ways in which the spy novel can function as a medium for the exploration of serious themes. However, the cynicism which some critics consider to be a shared characteristic is, in fact, much more pronounced in Conrad and Greene than in le Carré. The social contract, as presented in Conrad's novels, is nothing better than a necessary evil, while Greene rejects it entirely. Le Carré, on the other hand, although scathing in his analysis of the contemporary situation, offers an ideal of the well-ordered society in which a proper balance is achieved between the claims of the group and those of the individual.

As le Carré's optimism about the potential value of the

---

[11] T. J. Binyon, 'A Gentleman Among Players', *Times Literary Supplement*, 9 Sept. 1977, p. 1069.

social contract pulls him away from Conrad and Greene, so it draws him closer to writers in the popular tradition of the spy novel, for what he posits as an ideal, they proclaim as reality. In its basic formulas and overall structure, the fiction of Le Queux, Buchan, Oppenheim and others, is a restatement, within a specific social context, of the mythic quest story. It is characterized by a tripartite structure of separation, testing and reintegration that expresses, in terms applicable to the British situation, the general mythic affirmation of the ability of individual and society to enter into a mutually beneficial relationship.

Exactly how le Carré reconciles the diverse influences operating on him can be gauged most accurately by means of a structural comparison of the writers under consideration. In their novels, Conrad and Greene either invert or reject the conventions of the espionage novel, thereby proclaiming a fundamental disagreement with its assumptions. Le Carré, on the other hand, while also reformulating a number of important conventions, creates an overall pattern of action that overlaps quite significantly with the orthodox one. The effect is like that of taking a very familiar transparency and laying on top of it another that matches it in many ways but which blurs or obliterates some important lines. It is at those points, where blurring or obscuring occurs, that le Carré is exploring the gap between the mythic vision of man's relationship to society and the more cynical analysis of the modern condition, associated with Conrad and Greene. His technique is, in essence, much the same as that employed by Joyce in *Ulysses* or Eliot in *The Waste Land* in that they, too, judge twentieth-century society by how far it falls short of a mythic ideal, supplied for them by the *Odyssey* and the grail legend respectively.

Le Carré's novels are characterized by a double vision which is apparently created out of a combination of elements from the satirical and realistic espionage fiction of Conrad and Greene and the mythopoeic popular spy thrillers of writers such as Le Queux and Buchan. However, my discussion of le Carré as a spy novelist will conclude by suggesting that some of the darker implications of spying are expressed, if only in embryo, by a number of works from the popular tradition, leaving us with the intriguing possibility that less established authors were responsible for suggesting both aspects of the complex vision that sets le Carré above all previous writers of espionage fiction.

## I

Conrad's influence on le Carré is wide-ranging and goes beyond the boundaries of the present topic. Novels such as *Heart of Darkness* and *Lord Jim* not only point a direction for le Carré's experiments in technique, particularly for the series of subjective accounts out of which the total narratives of *Tinker, Tailor, Soldier, Spy* and *The Honourable Schoolboy* are constructed, but they also develop a number of themes which overlap with le Carré's major concerns. The naive and sentimental dichotomy so fundamental to le Carré's world-view is, for example, anticipated by the conflict between nature and civilization in *Heart of Darkness*. The debt le Carré owes to Conrad is particularly evident in the similar efforts made by Marlow and Smiley to find a resolution to impossible dilemmas in work, 'restraint'[12] – rephrased as 'moderation' (*TT*, XXIII, 207) by Smiley – and the companionship of fellow professionals.

The influence of *Lord Jim*, in which Conrad explores the problems inherent in accommodating heroic ideals to the

[12] Joseph Conrad, *Heart of Darkness* (New York: Norton, 1963), p. 68.

harsh realities of daily living, is equally direct. In particular, Conrad's dreamer Jim, and the pragmatic but sympathetic Marlow provide models for Prideaux and Smiley, and Westerby and Smiley, the characters through whom le Carré works out his version of this conflict in *Tinker, Tailor, Soldier, Spy* and *The Honourable Schoolboy.* The Marlow-Jim relationship also raises important questions about the nature of masculine friendship, particularly as it mimics the father-son bond, and as such bears a significant resemblance to Smiley's relationship with Jerry Westerby.

Our attention on this occasion, however, must be more narrowly focused on Conrad and le Carré as spy novelists and, in particular, on the part played by *The Secret Agent* in shaping le Carré's approach. He acknowledges his indebtedness to this novel by making allusions to two of its central images. In *Tinker, Tailor, Soldier, Spy,* Smiley concludes that a piece of modern sculpture describes nothing but a state of 'cosmic muddle' (XXVII, 229), and thereby recalls Conrad's description of Stevie's drawings as 'a rendering of cosmic chaos'.[13] Similarly, the reaction of the policeman who vomits at the sight of Vladimir's shattered face in *Smiley's People* (III, 36) mirrors that of the park keeper who 'was sick as a dog' at the sound of the shovel scraping up Stevie's body after the bomb explosion in *The Secret Agent* (87). This second allusion is particularly pointed because for le Carré and Conrad the act of vomiting serves to reintroduce a human response into scenes in which individuals have been sacrificed to the requirements of inhuman systems (anarchism in *The Secret Agent* and communism in *Smiley's People*).

The most important lesson which Conrad has to teach le

---

[13] *The Secret Agent* (Edinburgh: John Grant, 1925), p. 45. Subsequent references to *The Secret Agent* will be cited in the text.

Carré in *The Secret Agent* concerns the value of the spy novel form as a source for the metaphors which each author requires to give concrete and dramatic expression to the abstract conflict between nature and civilization. Of these metaphors, the most significant is spying itself which, in Conrad's hands, as later in le Carré's, comes to stand as a symbol for some of the more negative aspects of civilization. Espionage, and the associated activity, terrorism, is characterized in *The Secret Agent* by a denial of value to feeling, an overriding concern with 'facts' (25), a dependence on tehnique, and a subordination of the individual to larger goals. It allows Conrad to explore what happens when the tendency of civilization to cultivate efficiency and order and to be suspicious of the anarchy of emotion is taken to extremes.

The main burden of Conrad's analysis is borne by the experience of an individual spy, Verloc. Like so many of le Carré's spies he has turned to espionage after a youthful emotional disappointment, because it provides him with a sphere of activity in which he can concern himself with facts, matters of policy and institutions rather than with feelings or individuals. The habit of mind demanded by his profession comes to possess Verloc so completely that even his relationship with his wife lacks any but institutional dimensions: 'Mr Verloc loved his wife as a wife should be loved – that is, maritally, with the regard one has for one's chief possession' (179). The fact that Winnie is intensely and complexly human can be of no interest to a man who has given over his entire self to the role of secret agent: 'She was mysterious, with the mysteriousness of living beings. The far-famed agent Δ of the late Baron Stott-Wartenheim's alarmist despatches was not a man to break into such mysteries' (179–80).

Conrad supplements his portrait of Verloc with that of the Professor who has, if anything, gone even further in denying value to the emotions or the individual. Lacon's assertion that 'morality was method' (*TT*, X, 73) describes the Professor's attitudes better than it does those of any of le Carrés spies, for he is completely caught up with questions of technique, the most important being how to make 'a perfect detonator' (69). Thus, when he hears of the Greenwich disaster his mind is immediately occupied, not with thoughts of the hideous death, as he believes, of his old acquaintance Verloc, but with the possible cause of the premature explosion of his incendiary device (75–6).

Conrad's conclusions about the consequences for the individual of such a total acceptance of the values of espionage, and hence by implication, of civilization, are remarkably close to le Carré's. With the sacrifice of his ability to feel, a man such as Verloc also loses his sense of identity. Consequently, if he is to relate to the world around him he must assume a role, as an actor does. This acting metaphor which is, of course, also prominent in le Carré's analysis of the spy's situation (see my discussion of Charlie in chapter 5), is used most effectively when Verloc while boasting about his oratorical powers, reduces himself to a voice – that is, a medium for performing parts: 'His voice, famous for years at open-air meetings and at workmen's assemblies in large halls, had contributed, he said, to his reputation as a good and trustworthy comrade. It was, therefore, a part of his usefulness' (23).

The final irony in the situation of a man who is willing to merge the self into civilization in order to escape the dangerous world of feeling is for Conrad, as it is for le Carré, that he does not even gain the control that he anticipates. The world will not conveniently shrink itself to suit Verloc's limited frame of reference, and he is therefore helpless to cope with the operations of those parts of reality he tries to ignore. The potential for victimization inherent in this situation is dramatically realized in the events following the Greenwich explosion. Winnie's deeply emotional response to the death of her beloved brother, Stevie, falls outside Verloc's area of comprehension. As a result he is blind to her rapidly mounting hysteria and persists in making inappropriate and tactless comments until she kills him.

In his choice of Stevie, the simpleton who lives almost entirely through emotion and sensation and has little grasp of social reality, as a counterbalance to Verloc and the world of spying and by implication, to civilization itself, Conrad also provides a model, albeit a rather extreme one, for le Carré. In developing Stevie as a symbol of the natural state, Conrad anticipates much of what le Carré communicates through Shamus, Ann, Camilla, the orphan and Tatiana (whose insanity brings her particularly close to Stevie's experience of pure sensation). In part, Stevie's function is to bring into even sharper focus the deficiencies of Verloc and his kind, for through Stevie, as le Carré does through Shamus, Conrad asserts that feeling is the basis of all knowledge. Only Stevie. for instance, has the capacity to understand what is right and just. The world in general, let alone extreme examples of dehumanization such as Verloc and the Professor, simply accepts the fact of the 'maimed' cab driver and his 'infirm horse' (156). Stevie, on the other hand, because 'he felt with greater completeness and some profundity' (171), perceives that their situation constitutes an indictment of all the cruelty, injustice and inequity inherent in the civilized state of being: 'It was a bad world. Bad! Bad!' (171).

However, Conrad's main reason for introducing the character of Stevie is to emphasize, again as le Carré does, that neither the civilized, nor the natural state is adequate in itself. While Verloc's cultivation of the ethics of spying results in his ultimate destruction, Stevie's inability to deal with 'mere facts' (168) makes him an easy victim for those that can. Verloc thus has little difficulty in channelling Stevie's inchoate mass of emotion and sensation in such a way that he agrees to strike out against injustice by carrying a bomb up to the Greenwich Observatory. A stumble on the way and he experiences a death even more violent than Verloc's.

In *The Secret Agent* the emphasis is purely satirical; in the preface, the author describes his approach as 'ironic' (xii). Therefore, it has no need for a character such as Marlow who, in *Heart of Darkness,* functions as a mediator between the jungle (nature) on one side and the forces of colonialism (civilization) on the other. Because of this limitation, *The Secret Agent* provides only a partial model for le Carré who almost always includes a character in his novels, usually Smiley, who attempts to reconcile the naive with the sentimental. Nevertheless, because of the way in which it transforms spying into a metaphor for civilization, *The Secret Agent* has clearly exerted a considerable influence on the development of le Carré's own symbolic method.

Conrad further influenced le Carré by suggesting in *The Secret Agent* that spying is, in some significant ways, also a representation of society as it already is. For example, the pattern of images, through which le Carré establishes that secrecy is as much a characteristic of the overt world as it is of the secret, is derived quite directly from *The Secret Agent.* As Avrom Fleishman points out, the word 'secret' is used more than fifty times during the novel, the occurrences being divided about equally between references to Verloc and his profession and 'human states of being, emotions, conditions, and moral qualities: "secret ardor", "secret scorn", "secretly much affected", "secret griefs", "secretly outspoken thoughts", "secrecy of his heart", "secret liberation", "secret weakness", "secret fear", "secret of good nature", "secret of guilty breasts", "secret habits of mind"'.[14] The most crucial of all the secrets in *The Secret Agent* turns out to have nothing to do with espionage, but is rather the secret upon which the Verlocs' marriage is based: Winnie does not love her husband and has married to ensure Stevie's security.

A society which has been so thoroughly infiltrated by secrets is one, Conrad is suggesting, in which the community's emotional capacity has atrophied to such an extent that feeling human intercourse is no longer possible, and personal relationships have come to resemble those which are appropriate only in the realms of espionage. His point is much the same as that made by le Carré when, for instance, he describes the network of secrets that Thursgood believes must be kept if the small world of his school is to preserve at least an appearance of stability.

The espionage subculture is further reflected in Conrad's demonstrations of its methods as they are revealed in other social institutions. Police work in *The Secret Agent*, for example, displays an obsession with secrecy and emphasizes technique at the expense of feeling or concern for the individual. Both of these tendencies are particularly evident in Chief Inspector Heat. The keeping of secrets is a fundamental part of his approach to detection. Not even his superiors are aware, for example, that for several years Verloc has been employed as his informant, and during the investigation into Stevie's death, Heat goes so far as to conceal a vital clue until it is forced from him by the Assistant Commissioner.

Heat's reaction to the sight of Stevie's bloody remains indicates the extent to which, for the police, the demands of technique have displaced human concern. Heat is shocked by Stevie's death and he empathizes intensely with

---

[14] *Conrad's Politics: Community and Anarchy in the Fiction of Joseph Conrad* (Baltimore: The Johns Hopkins Press, 1967), p. 190.

the moment of excruciating pain that he imagines must have been felt between explosion and death. These feelings, however, have no bearing on his performance as the Chief Inspector who brings 'his trained faculties as an excellent investigator' (88) to bear on the situation. Thus, Heat the policeman views the body on the table 'with a calm face and the slightly anxious attention of an indigent customer bending over what may be called the by-products of a butcher's shop with a view to an inexpensive Sunday dinner' (88).

This technique has obviously had a significant influence on le Carré. In *A Small Town in Germany* he draws parallels between the ethics and attitudes of diplomacy and those of espionage. And in a number of novels, most notably *Call for the Dead, Tinker, Tailor, Soldier, Spy* and *The Honourable Schoolboy* he points to similarities between the spy and the government administrator.

For le Carré, the mirroring of the espionage subculture in society at large is completed by the creation of symbolic landscapes that possess those same soulless qualities. *The Secret Agent* has also played a significant part in the development of this technique, as is made clear by Conrad's recollection of the novel's imaginative evolution: 'Then the vision of an enormous town presented itself, of a monstrous town more populous than some continents and in its man-made might as if indifferent to heaven's frowns and smiles; a cruel devourer of the world's light' ('Author's Note', *The Secret Agent*, p. xii). Not only does the London of *Call for the Dead, The Looking-Glass War, Tinker, Tailor, Soldier, Spy* and *Smiley's People* possess these qualities of spiritual emptiness and darkness but it is created in a similar way through an accumulation of apparently trivial but in fact highly significant details. Conrad's method is seen as its best when he manages to infuse a brief account of the eccentric numbering of

London streets with complex undertones of disorder, concealed purpose and devious bureaucratic process (14–15). Le Carré achieves something almost as impressive in his transformation of a description of the bell-pushes on a house in Lock Gardens into a paradigm for the process of social change and disintegration (*TT*, XXXVI, 317).

Conrad and le Carré's approach to description is so similar that passages from their novels often have a close resemblance. The following paragraph, for example, in which Conrad uses detail to create a sense of the constricted, blind, confused, alienated and abandoned nature of London, clearly recalls the three passages with which I began my analysis in chapter 2:

> In order to reach sooner the point where he could take his omnibus, he turned brusquely out of the populous street into a narrow and dusky alley paved with flagstones. On one side the low brick houses had in their dusty windows the sightless, moribund look of incurable decay – empty shells awaiting demolition. From the other side life had not departed wholly as yet. Facing the only gas-lamp yawned the cavern of a second-hand-furniture dealer, where, deep in the gloom of a sort of narrow avenue winding through a bizarre forest of wardrobes, with an undergrowth tangle of table legs, a tall pier-glass glimmered like a pool of water in a wood. An unhappy, homeless couch, accompanied by two unrelated chairs, stood in the open. (82)

## II

Like *The Secret Agent*, and often in similar ways, Graham Greene's spy novels provide a model for le Carré, both in the themes they explore and the methods they employ. For Greene, as for Conrad and later le Carré, the world of espionage provides opportunities to explore the tendency of social arrangements to exclude consideration of individual emotional needs. The precise nature of this exploration is revealed by a consideration of the double perspective on spying that he adopts in his four major spy novels, *The Confidential Agent, The Quiet American, Our Man in Havana* and *The Human Factor*. In each work Greene establishes on the one hand, that the values of spying are antithetical to everything that lends individual human life its dignity and purpose, but on the other, and very ironically, that the espionage subculture is in some significant ways a microcosm of modern society.

The first aspect of Greene's analysis is developed through a series of conflicts between his heroes and the espionage establishment. Each of the four heroes we will be considering, D., Fowler, Wormold and Castle, achieves personal dignity and complete humanity because he either learns or affirms that only the self and love can provide a proper centre of value. An essential part of the process by which he arrives at this conclusion is the rejection of espionage with its commitment to large, abstract and national rather than specific personal goals.

The pattern is established in Greene's earliest spy novel, *The Confidential Agent*. Initially, spying appeals to D. as an activity suitable for a man who has lost his ability to feel but who, nevertheless, possesses 'a sense of duty' (30). He soon learns, however, that those who are trained to be treacherous in their personal dealings tend also to be disloyal in their national affiliations, and his career as a spy yields nothing more than a series of betrayals which leave him feeling frustrated and ineffectual. D. concludes from this experience that all productive human activity must have a stable centre and gradually he diverts his energies away from his secret mission and towards Rose Cullen, with whom he experiences a gradual rebirth of emotion. At the moment of complete union with Rose, it seems to D. that a sense of purpose has been restored to a world that had appeared 'monstrous' and without 'superintending design' (215) while he was a spy: 'He felt no desire, and no claim: happiness was all about them on the small vibrating tramp [steamer]. To the confidential agent trust seemed to be returning into the violent and suspicious world' (286).

Fowler's exposure to the world of espionage in *The Quiet American* not only confirms for him the importance of the individual and of emotional life but also reveals their vulnerability. Prior to his meeting with the CIA agent, Pyle, Fowler has always pursued an ideal of love, but without much energy. As a result he repeatedly terminates relationships rather than struggling with the problems that they create. Pyle, however, causes a dramatic shift in Fowler's level of commitment by introducing him to a view of experience that is at once alien and threatening. For Pyle, what matters are general and essentially abstract notions of national purpose, and he is ever willing to sacrifice the individual to his conviction that Vietnam will benefit from the introduction of an American Third Force into its war with France. This is illustrated most dramatically by the killing of innocent civilians which is the result of a bombing organized by Pyle to advance American interests. Fowler is acutely aware of the implications of this incident, but of more immediate personal significance to him is Pyle's attempt to entice Phuong away from him on the grounds that she will be better off as an American housewife. Faced with evidence of the destructive power of Pyle's abstract approach to experience, Fowler at last realizes the need for an active commitment to the things he values. Thus, both to halt Pyle's political activities and to regain Phuong, he conspires in the murder of the American agent. This assertion of the value of the individual and personal relationships in the face of the threat posed by the dehumanized ethics of American intelligence robs Fowler of his peace of mind, but it also makes him more completely human. As Heng tells him, 'Sooner or later . . . one has to take sides. If one is to remain human' (194).

For Wormold, the hero of *Our Man in Havana,* the Secret Service is initially attractive because it offers financial security. However, he soon realizes that involvement in espionage leads inevitably to dehumanization and the experience of absurdity. The casual manner in which British agents destroy Dr Hasselbacher's life-sustaining dreams revolts Wormold, and he is filled again and again with a sense of the detachment of spying, and the associated world of politics, from everything he considers 'real'. For Wormold, 'the evening hour' spent with his beloved daughter Millie is 'real, but not Hawthorne, mysterious and absurd, not the cruelties of police-stations and governments' (30). The essential absurdity of a way of life that takes no account of immediate personal experience, and proceeds instead according to general theories and firm assumptions, becomes most marked for Wormold in the ease with which he is able to pass off his vacuum-cleaner sketches as the plans of a secret weapon to a British Secret Service which has already decided that such a weapon must exist. Inevitably, Wormold arrives at the conclusion that, dangerous as he knows such a policy to be – his ability to love has been rewarded only by a wife who has deserted him and a daughter he is afraid to lose – he must function in accordance with his emotions and seek fulfilment in personal relationships: 'If I love or if I hate, let me love or hate as an individual. I will not be 59200/5 in anyone's global war' (206). From this point on Wormold refuses to 'believe in anything bigger than a home, or anything vaguer than a human being' (240). As a practical consequence of this shift in attitude, he turns away from his secret commitments and pledges himself instead to the pursuit of his love for Beatrice.

For Castle in *The Human Factor* there is never any doubt about the relative value to be attached to personal relationships and espionage. Whereas his love for his wife Sarah brings him complete fulfilment and great happiness, he regards the ways of the Secret Service as essentially immoral and foolish because they take no account of 'the human factor'. Its limitations emerge with particular clarity during the investigation into Davis's suspected treachery. Suspicion initially falls on Davis rather than Castle because Colonel Daintry automatically assumes that a Reading University graduate is less trustworthy than an Oxford man. The investigation is conducted with a similar lack of concern for the actual circumstances of the case, with the result that the authorities inevitably come to believe that they have proven what they were always sure was the truth. At this point, a situation made absurd by the limitations of the generalizing mind becomes hideous. Considerations of national security so far outweigh any concern for individual rights that, rather than suffer the possible embarrassment of a trial, Sir John Hargreaves and Dr Percival conspire to murder Davis.

Castle's scorn for espionage is so great and his commitment to the realm of personal experience so complete that he is even willing to give away British secrets to the Russians as a way of paying off a personal debt to the communist agent who helped Sarah to escape from South Africa. Such behaviour, which is usually ranked amongst the most despicable of crimes, seems entirely acceptable to Greene, and thus contained within his presentation of Castle is a very complete affirmation of belief in the primacy of individualistic ethics. If Greene finds anything tragic in Castle's eventual exile in Moscow, it is not that he has lost his country, but that his separation from Sarah may be final.

These novels, then, work together to advance a single thesis: human life becomes meaningful only when individuals allow themselves to be guided by emotions and seek fulfilment in personal relationships. The qualitative difference between the personal and the espionage worlds is perhaps best summed up by the different types of secrecy which, it is suggested in *The Human Factor,* are characteristic of each. Castle's relationship with Sarah is secret in that they share knowledge denied to the rest of the world: 'Endearments – dear and darling – were everyday currency to be employed in company, but a name was strictly private, never to be betrayed to a stranger outside the tribe. At the height of love she would cry aloud his secret tribal name' (83). In this context, secrecy plays a vital role in creating the special kind of intimacy that lies at the root of the love relationship, and is thus part of the process by which individuals draw closer together. In the context of espionage, however, secrets are kept in order that one set of people might enjoy an advantage over another, and therefore become synonymous with suspicion, divisiveness and alienation.

With the exception of *The Human Factor* which ends with the reunion of Castle and Sarah still in doubt, Greene's spy novels are comedies in which the individualistic hero triumphs over the life-denying forces of espionage. Nevertheless, there is a central irony to be found in each of them. Having clearly established that the espionage world functions in a way that is antithetical to everything that gives life its dignity and purpose, Greene then suggests that in many respects society at large is organized along similar lines.

The major technique used by Greene to develop the microcosmic implications of espionage is symbolic description. Except in *The Confidential Agent,* where he draws a rather complete picture of the British urban scene, Greene uses description sparingly. His technique can be seen at its most successful, however, in the description of the station at Willing, as D. waits for the train to Benditch in *The Confidential Agent*. The setting itself, a deserted railway platform on a cold Sunday morning before dawn, creates a powerful sense of spiritual *malaise*:

> It was still dark over the whole quiet Midland country-side. The small unimportant junction lay lit up like a centre-piece in a darkened shop window; oil lamps burned beside the General Waiting Room, an iron foot-bridge straddled across towards another smoky flame, and the cold wind took the steam out of the engine and flapped it back along the platform. It was Sunday morning. (211)

The scene gains its particular poignancy from the sense of loss with which Grene infuses almost every detail. Just as 'the tail-light of the train moved on like a firefly and was suddenly extinguished in some invisible tunnel' (211), so we are made to feel that this is a world that was once light but which has now sunk into permanent darkness. The promise of dawn seems to belong to another place: 'He went outside; it was still pitch dark beyond the little platform, but you were aware that somewhere there was light' (216). Morning does of course finally come but it reveals nothing to D. but ugliness and further darkness: 'The siding loomed slowly up with a row of trucks marked: "Benditch Collieries", the rails stretched out towards a fence, a dark shape which became a barn and then an ugly blackened winter field. Other platforms came into sight, shuttered and dead' (217). A clue to the source of this loss of illumination is provided by the dim waiting-room photograph of an idyllic love scene: 'a gentleman in a grey bowler and a Norfolk jacket was leaning over a handrail talking to a lady in a picture hat and white muslin' (213).

Love, Greene seems to be suggesting, has 'faded' (212) and now 'belonged to history' (213).

That this is indeed the significance of the photograph is confirmed by a number of other scenes in which sexual elements form an integral part of the landscape, not as an intimate bonding of two people, but as a source of financial transactions. When D., for example, is passing Marble Arch in the 'bitter cold', he sees that 'all down the road the cad cars waited for the right easy girls, and the cheap prostitutes sat hopelessly in the shadows' (186). Similarly, when Castle visits Raymond's Revuebar he observes the following dispiriting reduction of female sexuality to a display of meat for sale:

> The girl drank from a bottle of High and Dry suspended above the hammock on a string and after each swallow she removed a piece of clothing with an air of ginny abandon. At long last they could see her naked buttocks outlined by a net like the rump of a chicken seen through a Soho housewife's string bag. A party of businessmen from Birmingham applauded with some violence, and one man went so far as to wave a Diners Club card above his head, perhaps to show his financial standing (76–7).

Another of Greene's archetypically modern locations the Havana of *Our Man in Havana* is an 'eroded', 'smudged', 'featureless', 'shabby' place (54), which has as its chief commerce 'the sexual exchange'. In such a milieu 'one sold sex or one bought it – immaterial which, but it was never given away' (58).

Greene further establishes the espionage world as a microcosm by means of a number of brief evocations of other social institutions that display characteristics usually associated with spying. In *The Confidential Agent* Greene demonstrates that there is no place within capitalist enterprise, either from the point of view of the employers or the workers, for consideration of human needs. Thus, when it comes to making a decision about coal supplies to a country involved in civil war, D.'s personal pleas and the suffering of those caught up in the conflict carry little weight in the face of concerns about profits and wages.

The Catholic Church, as presented in *The Human Factor,* is no less insensitive to the individual, and the equation of espionage with Catholicism suggested by the character who claims that spies and priests are both involved in 'the hush-hush business' (212), proves to be quite accurate. Castle, a non-believer, is brought into the confessional by desperate loneliness. However, his plea for help is rejected because the priest is too obsessed with the proper forms of the confession (or, in spying terms, with technique) to respond spontaneously to an approach couched in uniquely personal terms (233–4).

The ways of espionage are also mirrored in the language school visited by D. in *The Confidential Agent.* Despite its official purpose, which is to foster universal communication and understanding, the operations of the school are infused with a deep sense of mistrust and the principal, Dr Bellows, even goes so far as to spy on his instructors: 'Once D. thought he heard Dr Bellows pass down the passage on rubber-soled shoes. There wasn't much trust even in the centre of internationalism' (58–9).

Much of the ground covered by Greene's spy novels has obviously already been explored by Conrad in *The Secret Agent.* Both are alert to the thematic possibilities provided by espionage as a subculture in which individual emotional imperatives are consistently made subservient to ideological generalizations and national goals and both work along similar lines to establish the microcosmic implications of spying. As a result, it is often difficult to say where Conrad's influence on le Carré ends and Greene's begins. However, there are areas in which le Carré owes a clear debt to Greene alone.

The Department in *The Looking-Glass War* is like the version of the Secret Service presented in *Our Man in Havana* in that its members are so fixated on larger goals that they pay little attention to actual circumstances. The Chief assumes that Cuba has secrets to yield up, and for Leclerc it is axiomatic that East Germany contains suitable targets for his agents; any information that falls into their hands is manipulated to conform to these presuppositions. Thus, smudged and blurred photographs are enough to convince Leclerc of the introduction of a new Russian rocket into East Germany and sketches of a vacuum-cleaner serve for the Chief as hard evidence of the existence of a secret weapon in Cuba. These incidents resemble each other sufficiently, in nature and function, to make it appear that le Carré had *Our Man in Havana* in mind when he wrote *The Looking-Glass War*. This is further suggested by the similar use Greene and le Carré make of childhood imagery to define the detachment from reality, and hence absurdity, of their respective secret agencies. For Beatrice in *Our Man in Havana*, Wormold is 'real' but the Secret Service is '*Boy's Own Paper*' (182), and for le Carré the Department in *The Looking-Glass War* is based on the world of 'children's magazines' (II, 25).

So similar are their descriptive techniques that it is impossible to be sure whether Conrad or Greene had the greater influence on le Carré's use of description. Certainly, any reader unfamiliar with *The Secret Agent* might think that le Carré had Greene's Willing Station, Dover and London very much in mind as he created his own English landscapes. There is, however, one scene in *The Confidential Agent* for which there is no possible precedent in Conrad. While trying to escape from England, D.

hides out at the Lido, a place which is remarkably similar in appearance and symbolic function to the motel visited by Prideaux and Smiley in *Tinker, Tailor, Soldier, Spy*. The most marked characteristic of each place is its insubstantiality. Passing traffic makes everything in the motel room rattle and Smiley can hear voices and music on each side and above him. Similarly, the Lido, which is advertised as 'a cruise on land' (269), seems barely anchored to the ground as it is battered by the wind: 'The clock tower, like the bridge of a ship, heaved among the clouds' (273). The walls of D.'s room are no less thin than Smiley's, and he too is engulfed in music and voices: 'There was a good deal of noise: the laughter which is technically known as happy, and several radios were playing, plugged into different stations; the walls were very thin; so that you could hear everything which went on in the neighbouring rooms – a man seemed to be flinging his shoes against the wall' (271). Implicit within the flimsiness of each place is a symbolic expression of the author's views on the quality of modern relationships. The privacy which forms the solid base for real intimacy, is, it seems, no longer available nor even desired. Instead intercourse between individuals has been reduced to a very public sharing of drink, food, talk and sex. Bonds formed in such circumstances, Greene and le Carré are suggesting, possess no more substance than the places in which they are created.

### III

Conrad and Greene have clearly had a profound influence on John le Carré. From them he has inherited not only a model of how espionage can be made to serve as a medium for exploring the conflict between self and civilization but also techniques for establishing the connectedness of the secret and overt worlds. However, similar as the three writers are in their approach to spy fiction, there are significant differences in the visions that emerge from their novels. These differences are to be found not so much in their analyses of the contemporary situation as in their broader assumptions about the relationship of individual to society. Conrad, Greene and le Carré are in general agreement that modern society, as its marked likedness to the world of espionage suggests, is essentially loveless and dehumanizing. However, whereas for Conrad and Greene such a denial of value to the individual is an inevitable consequence of organizing people into groups, for le Carré it is simply a characteristic of a society which has become decadent.

In Conrad's view truth is to be found within the dark unconscious areas of the human personality, but he also believes that the atavistic energies released by the irrational self are as destructive as they are creative. Whereas Stevie's instincts in *The Secret Agent* are the source of a profound sympathy with his fellow human beings, Winnie's drive her to the brutal slaughter of her husband. Society, with its rules, regulations, conventions and customs, its ideals of efficiency and progress, is therefore necessary in order that those primitive urges might be checked. However, so far as Conrad is concerned, having performed this function, the social organism has no further value because the ideological structures which it offers as a substitute for the instinctive truths suppressed in the cause of preventing mayhem provide the individual with only an appearance of purpose. As Jacques Berthoud puts it, society, as it appears in Conrad's novels, is at once 'indispensable' and 'indefensible'.[15]

---

[15] *Joseph Conrad: The Major Phase* (Cambridge: Cambridge University Press, 1978), p. 139. I am also greatly indebted to Ian Watt, *Conrad in the Nineteenth Century* (London: Chatto and Windus, 1980).

For Greene the emotions are an entirely creative force, the source of that ability to love out of which the most fulfilling of human bonds is created. Thus, whereas Conrad accepts the necessity of the social contract in spite of the loss of self that results from it, Greene rejects it entirely and directs his heroes to seek salvation within the realm of personal relationships.

Le Carré disagrees with Conrad and Greene about the kind of relationship that can exist between the individual and his society because he has a rather different view of human personality. For him truth derives not just from feeling, important as that is, but from a reconciliation of the claims of the emotional and the rational (or the naive and the sentimental) aspects of the self. The conflict between these two forces is so great, however, that a person has little hope of forcing them into any kind of harmony. Consequently, le Carré believes that society can perform a vital function if it is able to develop structures which allow scope for the expression of, as Schiller puts it, 'not merely the objective and generic but also the subjective and specific'[16] poles of the personality, and thereby provide a context within which the individual can further an impulse towards wholeness.

Le Carré's novels are, then, informed by an ideal of unity between self and society that is alien to Conrad or Greene. This fundamental difference in vision is revealed to some extent by the evocation of well-balanced societies of the past contained within le Carré's architectural allusions (see chapter 2) and his analysis of the class system and polite codes of eighteenth- and nineteenth-century England (see chapter 1). However, it can be brought into particularly sharp focus by extending our analysis of le

---

[16] Friedrich Schiller, *On the Aesthetic Education of Man*, trans. Reginald Snell (New York: Ungar, 1965), p. 32.

Carré's place within the tradition of the spy novel into the realm of structure.

The popular spy novel, as critics have often pointed out, follows a pattern of action which closely resembles that to be found in myth stories.[17] The underlying structure in each case is a three-part one of separation, testing and reintegration, and there is a great similarity between the major recurring characters and functions, to use Propp's term, of the two forms. A brief comparison should suffice to demonstrate this. The essential myth story, according to the analyses of both Propp and Campbell,[18] is made up of the following functions (labelled A–H for purposes of comparison). The hero becomes aware of an act of villainy or perceives a lack in himself or society (A). He then journeys forth with the intention of correcting the situation (B). His journey takes him into strange and uncharted territory where he encounters magical helpers and hinderers (C), and is tested in various ways (D). The climactic test involves him in a battle with the villain (E). Having defeated the villain, he reaches the goal of his quest (F) and returns home to restore order to his kingdom (G). The hero is typically rewarded with a royal marriage (H).

The basic plot of the spy novel, as defined by Eco's study of Fleming, Usborne's of Buchan and Sapper, Harper's of Buchan, and Merry's more general analysis of the form,

[17] See, for example, Umberto Eco, 'The Narrative Structure in Fleming', in *The Bond Affair*, ed. Oreste de Bueno and Umberto Eco (London: MacDonald, 1966), pp. 35–75; Ralph Harper, *The World of the Thriller* (Cleveland: Case Western Reserve University, 1969); Bruce Merry, *Anatomy of the Spy Thriller* (Montreal: McGill-Queen's University Press, 1977); Lars Ole Sauerberg, 'The Novel of Espionage: An Attempt at Generic Criticism', *Pre-Publications of the English Institute of Odense University*, 9 (Sept. 1977), pp. 1–15; Richard Usborne, *Clubland Heroes* (London: Constable, 1953).
[18] Vladimir Propp, *Morphology of the Folktale*, 2nd edn. (Austin: University of Texas Press, 1968); Joseph Campbell, *The Hero with a Thousand Faces* (New York: Pantheon, 1949).

takes an almost identical course. The agent-hero either stumbles on or is informed by his control of a threat to national security posed by a hostile power (A). He then either takes it on himself or is ordered to counter this threat and sets out on his mission (B) into enemy territory where he is often assisted by fellow agents or a sympathetic girl and is always threatened by representatives of the enemy (C). After various tests of his intelligence, ingenuity and physical courage (D), he battles with and defeats the villain (E). This is either the goal of his quest or brings him to the goal (F). Finally, he returns home (G) and is rewarded with a decoration, promotion or marriage (H).

The function of myth, according to Joseph Campbell, who is deeply influenced by Jung's theory of the collective unconscious and by the structural similarities between myth and ritual, is to provide a symbolic affirmation of the individual's ability to move successfully from one stage of life to another and of the ability of social structures to accommodate and facilitate the transition.[19] This theme is brought into sharpest focus by the battle with the villain. Since the villain represents both the dark side of the hero's own personality and a set of values alien to his society, his defeat and the completion of the quest which follows is an equally strong confirmation of the worth of individual and group. Their final relationship is inevitably a close one and the bond created between them is clearly marked by the hero's entry through marriage into the ruling family.

The spy novel became popular in Britain during the early years of this century because, as John Cawelti argues is the case with all the great popular genres,[20] it reaffirmed in terms acceptable to the society of the day the continued

[19] Campbell, *The Hero with a Thousand Faces*, pp. 10–11.
[20] *Adventure, Mystery and Romance: Formula Stories as Art and Popular Culture* (Chicago: University of Chicago Press, 1976), p. 6.

efficacy of mythic ideals. According to David Stafford, such a confirmation of the worth of British society was particularly needed during this period because, for the first time since Waterloo, the established order was under siege from new social and political forces at home and from the emergence of powerful enemies abroad.[21] Thus, the typical hero in the novels of Childers, Le Queux, Hill and Offin, the earliest practitioners of the form, is a member of the British ruling class who commits himself completely to the cultivation of its gentlemanly ideals. His mission brings him up against an antagonist, usually a member of the French or German Secret Service or the British working class, who, because of his ignorance of the rules of fair play, hunnish personal habits or anarchist tendencies, offers a challenge not just to the hero, but to the values of his society. By defeating him, therefore, the hero proves both his own worth and the superiority of British society. His adventures are brought to an end with a promotion or marriage symbolic of the condition of mutual harmony into which hero and society have entered.

Neither the general optimism of myth nor the spy novel's specific assertion of faith in the workings of British society can have had much appeal for Conrad and Greene. For them, social grouping, by its very nature, dimishes rather than enhances an individual's chances of personal fulfilment, and both cite Britain as a particularly oppressive example of the way in which social forces operate. As a way of emphasizing their disagreement with the mythic vision of the spy novel, Conrad and Greene set out to subvert the usual formulas and structure of the genre.

Conrad deviates most fundamentally from the norms of the spy novel in both the type of hero he creates and in the

[21] 'Spies and Gentlemen: The Birth of the British Spy Novel, 1893–1914', *Victorian Studies*, 24 (Summer 1981), pp. 489–509.

nature of the mission in which he involves him. The questing hero is a figure that usually exerts a strong influence on Conrad's imagination, as we can see from his depiction of Lord Jim or Nostromo and, to some extent, Marlow in *Heart of Darkness*. However, in *The Secret Agent* he offers as his protagonist the distinctly unheroic figure of Verloc. Slothful by nature and lacking any sense of noble purpose, Verloc undertakes the mission around which *The Secret Agent* is organized only as a means of saving his own skin. He then proceeds to perform the tasks set him in a cowardly and ineffective way. Afraid to carry the bomb, he recruits his simple-minded brother-in-law, and by so doing sets in motion a train of events that ends in the tragi-farcical failure of the attempt to blow up the Greenwich Observatory.

Expressed through Verloc's personal inadequacies and unsuccessful quest is a rejection of the spy novel's more general mythic assertion of faith in the nature of the relationship between the individual and society. However, since he is working for a foreign power against Britain, they do not constitute a denial of its usual specific justification of British society. Such a denial *is* contained, however, in the relationship between Verloc and the two policemen, Inspector Heat and the Assistant Commissioner. Although Verloc is the protagonist in *The Secret Agent,* because he is the enemy of Britain his function, in terms of the usual conventions of the genre, is closer to that of villain than hero. Such a variation of the spy novel form, in which the enemy agent takes the initiative and penetrates British territory, is not uncommon. Ken Follett's *The Eye of the Needle* is a well-known recent example. The hero in this type of novel is the character who, like Follett's Lucy Rose, defends England against the enemy agent.

In *The Secret Agent* the duties of the hero fall on Heat

and the Assistant Commissioner, and it is in their failure to carry them out that Conrad makes clear the distinction between his vision of British society and that put forward in other spy novels. As I suggested earlier, the battle with the villain is, of all the functions in myth and espionage fiction, the one which establishes most clearly the worth of the hero and society. It is, therefore, extremely significant that this function is omitted from *The Secret Agent*. Heat and the Assistant Commissioner remain in complete ignorance of Verloc's plans and he would, in fact, have proceeded unhindered to his goal had it not been for his own incompetence. The two policemen do, of course, take on a more active role in the investigation which follows the explosion. However, even though they manage to identify Verloc as the person responsible, they fail once again to come to grips with him, and the role of villain-slayer is preempted by Verloc's wife, Winnie.

Through manipulation of three of the most important formulas of the genre – the character of the hero, the hero's quest and the battle with the villain – Conrad thus undercuts both the mythopoeic and the socially specific implications of the spy novel. Far from being a parable of how the society and its members can work towards a condition of mutual harmony, *The Secret Agent* demonstrates nothing more than the futility and alienation of individual life and the hopeless inadequacy of British society.

But these deviations from the norms of the spy novel do not reflect the full extent of Conrad's subversion of the genre. In order to talk about the novel as an ironic quest story, I have put back into chronological order events that are, in fact, presented in a rather different sequence. Thus, in *The Secret Agent,* the outcome of Verloc's mission is revealed, not as would be usual at the end of the action, but immediately after the scene in which he is assigned his task. The details of his quest emerge later in an anticlimatic reconstruction. Conrad's point in ordering events in such a way is to make the experience of reading his novel completely different from that of reading conventional spy fiction. In place of the gradual build-up of suspense and the dramatic climax created by the genre's typical structure, *The Secret Agent* offers only bathos. Conrad thus develops an unheroic form appropriate for a novel in which he is intent on undercutting the heroic vision.

Graham Greene employs similar techniques in his attempt to subvert the spy novel. His rejection of the genre's assumptions is most extreme in *The Quiet American*. Although the novel is concerned with spying, Greene pushes the subject into the background and focuses his attention on Fowler, the journalist, rather than Pyle, the CIA agent. Furthermore, lest, even in this subsidiary position, the unfolding of the espionage quest plot might create some tension and excitement, Greene, like Conrad, scrambles the chronological sequence of events and informs the reader at an early point of the agent's fate.

When this spy plot is disinterrred from where it has been buried by Greene, it soon becomes evident that its significance is quite different from the usual one. Pyle himself bears a clear resemblance to the typical hero of myth or espionage fiction in that he is brave, resourceful and deeply committed to the advancement of his nation's cause. The single-handed journey he makes up the river to Phat Diem is an enterprise cast in a truly heroic mould. However, through the negative light in which he presents American imperialism, Greene calls into question the worthiness of the very call to adventure that Pyle is answering. Consequently, in Greene's version of the quest story, the more diligently the hero seeks to embody within himself the ideals of his nation and the more gallantly he struggles to overthrow its enemies, the more disastrous the consequences. The only grounds for hope that such a story of dehumanization and exploitation can yield up are to be found not in any of Pyle's successes but in his eventual failure.

To make it clear that implicit within his espionage plot is a broad condemnation of the spy hero's nationalistic ideals and not just of Pyle's commitment to American ideology, Greene shapes the main action of his novel around an alternative quest. The hero of this quest is Fowler, a man we are asked to admire because, in authentic mythic style, he shakes off a debilitating apathy and answers the call to adventure. His cause, however, is entirely personal and as he journeys forth in defence of his own ideal of love he is setting himself, not just against the USA, but against Britain (with its demand that he remain committed to bourgeois marital and career ideals) and, by implication, against all nations. Thus, his opponent, Pyle, who inevitably assumes the role of villain in this quest story, represents more than the USA, and contained within Pyle's defeat is a general assertion of faith in the ability of the individual to triumph over the forces of nationalism, however they might manifest themselves.

The espionage plot is restored to a central position in *The Confidential Agent, Our Man in Havana,* and *The Human Factor,* but only so that Greene might offer a more direct challenge to its usual assumptions. The starting-point for this challenge is, in each case, a reworking of the convention which identifies the spy's goals with those of his country. Of Greene's three agents, only D. ever has any intention of completing the mission to which he is assigned. Thus, whereas D. struggles for some time to get the coal contracts his government needs, Wormold begins immediately to supply false information on Cuban rocket sites and Castle sabotages Operation Uncle Remus. Eventually, however, D. becomes disillusioned with his efforts and, like Wormold and Castle, begins to pursue personal goals that take him further and further from the official aims of his mission.

Because the conventional patterns of espionage fiction are firmly imprinted on these three novels, the reader who is familiar with the form is able to make a direct comparison between the fate which Greene's agents work out for themselves and that which they would have experienced had they followed through the line of action which they reject. As a result, we can see that while the spy's personal quest for love ends in enhanced dignity, a sense of purpose and renewed vitality, the espionage mission holds out a promise of nothing better than betrayal, dehumanization and the experience of absurdity. Implicit in this gap between the conclusions, actual and potential, of the spy's private and official missions is a clear rejection on Greene's part of the nationalistic ideology of espionage fiction.

Greene, then, structures *The Quiet American* around two quests and his other three novels around an actual and a potential quest. In each case, however, the double quest structure serves much the same purpose. On the one hand it enables Greene to debunk the ideology of espionage fiction and on the other to offer an alternative sphere of heroic action. Greene's structural relationship to the spy novel is therefore rather more complex than Conrad's, since the latter limits himself to attacking the norms of the genre. However, it is the common ground that Conrad and Greene share in their complete rejection of the fundamental assumptions upon which the spy novel form is based, that provides the most instructive basis for comparison with le Carré.

Of the ways in which le Carré reworks the formulas of spy fiction, four are particularly important. First, in le Carré's novels as in Greene's, there is almost always a discrepancy between the agent's goals and those of his control. Smiley, for instance, twice defies orders and becomes involved in a very different mission from the one prescribed. In *Call for the Dead*, Maston orders him to terminate his enquiries into Fennan's death, but Smiley continues with the investigation on a private basis. Similarly, in *Smiley's People*, instead of conducting the cover-up requested by Lacon and Enderby, he sets out to complete the mission in which Vladimir was involved at the time of his death. Turner, in *A Small Town in Germany*, also disobeys instructions and tries to solve the mystery of Harting's disappearance rather than simply ensure that it is not a source of embarrassment to the British government. In *The Looking-Glass War*, *The Spy Who Came in from the Cold*, *Tinker, Tailor, Soldier, Spy*, *The Honourable Schoolboy*, and *The Little Drummer Girl*, on the other hand, it is the control figures – Control in the first two instances, Lacon, Smiley, and Kurtz – who, to a greater or lesser extent, deceive their agents (Leiser, Leamas, Smiley, Westerby, and Charlie) about the nature of their missions or the spirit in which they should be approached. Control, for instance, conceals from Leamas that his apparent target, Mundt, is in fact working for the British, and both Lacon and Kurtz make hypocritical appeals, the one to Smiley's sense of duty and the other to Charlie's humanity.

Second, le Carré usually draws little or no moral distinction between hero and supposed villain. Harting in *A Small Town in Germany* and Drake Ko in *The Honourable Schoolboy* both prove to be decent and humane men whose activities are not even directed against the interests of British Intelligence. Others such as Dieter Frey in *Call for the Dead*, Fiedler in *The Spy Who Came in from the Cold*, Haydon in *Tinker, Tailor, Soldier, Spy*, Karla, at least in *Smiley's People*, and Khalil in *The Little Drummer Girl*, while obviously enemies, all reveal intensely human faces. Even Haydon, the arch-betrayer, is for Guillam, at the end of things, still 'only Bill and they had done a lot together' (*TT*, XXXVI, 329). The closing of the moral gap between hero and villain is most striking in those instances when the enemy provides the British agent with a lesson in humanity. Both Dieter Frey's conduct during their death struggle and Karla's commitment to his insane daughter, for instance, cause Smiley to question his own behaviour. Similarly, the more his investigations reveal Harting to be a vital and caring human being, the more Turner comes to realize the limitations of his own coldly analytical approach to experience.

Third, le Carré's heroes either fall short of the goal of their mission, are killed, or, having been made aware of the humanity of their antagonist, are dissatisfied with their success. Thus, Leiser is captured by the East Germans and Turner fails to apprehend Harting, while Westerby and Leamas are killed in the course of their espionage activities. Smiley (on a number of occasions), Prideaux (in that he eventually kills Bill Haydon) and Charlie complete the tasks set them but find more to mourn than to celebrate in the defeat of Frey, Haydon, Ko, Karla and Khalil.

Fourth, on those occasions when the hero is successful, the completion of the mission is not followed by his reintegration into society. Smiley is offered a new position in the Circus after the Fennan case but refuses it, and he is left alone and thoroughly alienated by his final victory over Karla. Prideaux returns to Thursgood's school (his retreat from the world) after killing Haydon. And Charlie's service with the Israelis convinces her that she does not want the home with them once promised to her. Only *Tinker, Tailor, Soldier, Spy* concludes in a way at all typical of the spy novel, in that Smiley becomes head of the Circus following his discovery of the identity of the mole Gerald. However, this reintegration is temporary, and the continuation of the story into *The Honourable Schoolboy* ends, despite further successes, in Smiley's forced resignation.

The combined effect of these deviations from the conventions of the espionage genre is to create a pattern of action in which there is a considerable degree of alienation of the individual from society. The various conflicts that exist between the control who, as is always the case in the spy novel, is the voice of social authority, and the agent suggest that both sides must take some responsibility for this division. Based on Control's behaviour in *The Looking-Glass War,* for instance, it would appear that British society has experienced some loss of moral integrity and respect for individual life. At the same time, the agent, Leiser, is so hopelessly anachronistic in his approach to experience that he is completely unfitted to deal with any version of contemporary reality. On the whole, though, the different attitudes revealed by the two parties to the mission indicate that the major flaws reside in the society rather than in the questing hero. For all their limitations, le Carré's agents consistently approach their missions in an unselfish, straightforward, responsible and loyal way, and in the course of them demonstrate a range of qualities including resourcefulness, intelligence, courage and even the ability to love. The control figures, on the other hand, except in part for Smiley in *The Honourable Schoolboy,* are devious, lacking in integrity, and often more concerned with personal gain or convenience than with the national good.

The suggestion that the inadequate ethics of the group, rather than individual limitations, lie at the root of their alienation from each other, is reinforced by le Carré's other reworkings of the conventions of espionage fiction which are outlined above. Those occasions on which the agent fails to achieve the goal of the mission and/or is killed, for instance, usually reflect worse on society. Leiser's naivety and the decisions made by Leamas and Westerby to put love ahead of national loyalties which have become distasteful to them are all, of course, factors which contribute to their failure and/or death. Nevertheless, they are unsuccessful primarily because they are sacrificed to the ignoble ends of their own side. Thus, Leiser dies to ensure Control's victory in a power struggle with Leclerc's Department, Leamas as a consequence of Control's concern to protect the despicable Mundt, and Westerby to appease the Americans and thereby advance Enderby's career.

Another of le Carré's variations on the standard formulas of spy fiction – the agent's lack of satisfaction with operations that are, in official terms, successful – further points up the limitations of society by emphasizing how much more complex is the agent's moral code than is that of the group. The death of Dieter Frey, the unmasking of Bill Haydon or the defection of Karla can be a source of unreserved celebration only for those whose concern is restricted to the fulfilment of narrowly defined national goals. For Smiley and others who are also conscious of the personal implications of such situations, they are a source more of anxiety and sorrow than of joy.

The most damning indictment of society, however, is contained within its failure to achieve any final harmony with those agents who have proven their worth by completing the tasks assigned them. Le Carré's point is much the same, regardless of whether it is the agent who turns away from involvement in society, or the society which is unwilling to accommodate the agent. The Circus, for instance, emerges with equal discredit on those occasions when Smiley follows his brilliant and heroic performance in the Fennan case by refusing to work for an organization run by the talentless bureaucrat Maston, and when he is forced into retirement, despite his success in Operation

Dolphin, in order that Enderby, a manipulative careerist inexperienced in espionage, might become head of the service.

The tendency of the novels to create a conflict between agent and secret service is greatly reinforced by the other major departure from the norms of espionage fiction: the lack of moral distinction between hero and supposed villain. Although often at odds with their own society, le Carré's agent-heroes are not in the least attracted by the ideology of the East German or the Russian enemy – Leamas, Prideaux and Smiley all speak out at various times against communism – and their gravitation towards the agent who represents East Germany or the Soviet Union is based on an admiration, not of his political beliefs, but of his personal qualities. Thus, a configuration of moral forces is created in which, rather than each being aligned with his society against the other agent and his society, as would be usual in the spy novel, the two individuals stand together against their nations.  .

These shifts in the use of three important conventions of the spy novel (A, E, F) and the complete absence of a fourth (G) create a significant gap between le Carré and writers such as Le Queux or Buchan, in whose novels agent and control, Hannay and Bullivant for example, are always united in purpose; the villain as well as his nation is completely evil; and the hero, having completed his mission in a way as pleasing to him as to his society, is rewarded with increased social prestige or, in *Mr Standfast* at least, marriage. We must be careful, however, not to over-estimate the width of this gap, for, much as he tends towards it, le Carré does not in fact rework the formulas of espionage fiction in such a way as to project a vision of total alienation.

Le Carré's relationship to the popular spy novel differs most markedly from that of Conrad and Greene in that he is always faithful to the usual sequence of functions. If le Carré rearranges his chronology, as he does in *Tinker, Tailor, Soldier, Spy,* it is in order to move the main espionage plot to centre stage and not, as would be the case with Conrad or Greene, to push it into the background. Thus, the novel begins with Smiley answering the call to adventure rather than with any of the crucial events, such as Haydon's manoeuvring of Alleline into power, Control's desperate attempts to discover the identity of the mole Gerald, or Prideaux's abortive excursion into Czechoslovakia, that occur earlier. This material is introduced gradually in a series of flashbacks, but in such a way that the reader's attention is never deflected from the hero as he moves towards the completion of his quest.

Neither does le Carré, in the final analysis, adopt an ironic attitude to the quest that he has placed at the centre of his novels. Much as he emphasizes the seedier aspects of espionage, he still accepts that the character of unusual potential (and all his agent-protagonists are in some way or other exceptional human beings) can find within the role of spy sufficient opportunities to grow into full heroic stature. This is in sharp contrast to Conrad and Greene, whose rejection of the conventions of espionage fiction takes as its starting-point the notion that only a person such as Verloc or Pyle, who is morally deficient, will commit himself to spying. Wormold, D. and other characters who possess the ability to become heroes inevitably turn away from espionage as part of their progress towards full humanity.

Le Carré is able to take this affirmative attitude to the agent and his mission because although, as I suggested earlier, he comes close to shifting the central conflict in his novels to one between individuals and societies, of whatever political colour, he does in fact finally assert that, for all its faults, the British way of life is preferable to the

communist alternative. Therefore, its preservation provides, if only marginally, a worthwhile sphere of activity
for a man of heroic capabilities. Smiley, for instance,
although always critical of Britain, remains committed to
its cause because for him there is a clear if fine moral
distinction between a nation which, despite many offences
against the ideal, acknowledges the individual's rights to
be free and one, such as the Soviet Union, for whom the
suppression of the individual in favour of the collective is a
fundamental philosophical tenet. Those of le Carré's
heroes, such as Westerby, who become sufficiently disillusioned with Britain to turn away from it completely, are
viewed sympathetically but are judged to be wrong.

Even in their endings, le Carré's plots are not quite so
distinct from those of popular spy novels as the consistent
failure, death or dissatisfaction of the hero and his final
alienation from society might seem to indicate. Viewed
from the agent's perspective, things certainly do turn out
poorly, but from an official point of view, that is, as
defined by the control, the missions in all of le Carré's
novels end quite conventionally in a British triumph. In
those cases where the agent falls short of his target or is
killed, it is because he has been sacrificed to the control's
concealed goals (as in *The Looking-Glass War* and *The Spy
Who Came in from the Cold*) or has diverged from the
official aim of his mission (as in *A Small Town in Germany*
and *The Honourable Schoolboy*). His failure is thus a
precondition for the realization of national objectives.
Similarly, Smiley's unhappiness at the end of his missions
results from their moral complexity and not from any lack
of success in carrying out his original intentions.

The structure of le Carré's novels is, then, based on
elements from both the major traditions of espionage
fiction. Conventions are reworked to communicate a vision
of the individual's alienation from society. Nevertheless,

underneath the bleak surface of these novels in which, because of a cynicism about national ideologies, the clear black–white conflict of popular spy fiction seems to have been reduced to a battle between shades of grey, or between 'half-angels' and 'half-devils' (*SP*, XV, 179), there can be found something which approximates to the conventional mythic quest pattern. Heroes still exist in le Carré's world, and they venture forth on missions which help preserve the dominance of Britain over its morally less worthy enemies. The synthesis of mythopoeic and realistic elements thereby created is of such a kind as to persuade the reader that le Carré is essentially a writer of failed myths. The motifs which le Carré takes from Buchan, Childers, Le Queux and their followers provide him with an ideal vision of the individual's relationship to society, and their Britain is for him something close to a Golden Age, a perfect past world that never quite existed but which we long to recreate. In shaping his own fiction around these motifs, le Carré is struggling to mimic the form of the popular novel and to equate his Britain with the perfect Britain that appears there. His sense of the limitations of contemporary reality is far too strong, however, for the equation ever to be completed and his novels always deviate towards the patterns to be found in the very different espionage novels of Conrad and Greene. The extent of his deviation from the ideal mythic structure is a precise measure of le Carré's discontent with the modern world.

In order to point up the mythopoeic dimensions of his novels, le Carré occasionally introduces motifs from folklore and legend. Smiley's heroic function is, for instance, underlined by references to him as 'King Richard' (*SP*, XV, 178), to Guillam as his 'cupbearer' (*HS*, III, 51), and to his final pursuit of Karla as a 'lonely quest' (*SP*, XII, 128). However, le Carré shapes these allusions in such a way that, as with the structure of his novels, they do not ultimately fulfil their mythic promise. Smiley, for example, although triumphant over Karla at the end of *Smiley's People*, is not successful when their conflict is viewed within the context of the novel's folklore imagery. Then Karla, whom Vladimir dubs 'the Sandman' after a character in a German fairy tale because 'anyone who comes too close to him has a way of falling asleep' (XV, 182), is transformed into death, an enemy that, even with the help of 'the magician' (I, 25), the now clearly ageing Smiley cannot hope to defeat any more than could Gilgamesh or Bergman's knight before him. Given the impossible nature of his task, Smiley is more accurately equated with 'Childe Rowland' (*SP*, XXI, 255), the hero of Browning's ironic reworking of the Grail legend, than with the knights of epic romance. A similar use is made of folklore in *Call for the Dead* and *The Honourable Schoolboy*. *Call for the Dead* assigns Smiley the role of the frog who seeks in vain for 'the kiss that would turn him into a Prince' (I, 9), and the Fennan case is described as a version of 'Goldilocks' in which 'all three principals ... have now been eaten by bears' (XVI, 130). In *The Honourable Schoolboy*, Westerby is both a 'Dick Whittington' (V, 102) who finds the streets of London paved with false hopes, and a 'St George' (VI, 124) who is consumed by the dragon.

## IV

Up to this point I have argued that le Carré draws equally on the popular and cynical traditions of espionage fiction to create a version of the form expansive and complex enough to accommodate realistic and mythopoeic elements. Given his clearly demonstrable indebtedness to Conrad and Greene for the techniques needed to develop the realistic possibilities of the genre, there is perhaps no reason even to consider modifying this proposition. However, I would like to conclude by considering the intriguing possibility that his original inspiration might have been entirely provided by certain popular spy novelists whose work suggests, at least in embryo, the form's rich possibilities.

The novels of Le Queux, Buchan, Childers, Offin, Sapper and Oppenheim offer, of course, a simple and affirmative view of the world in general and of spying in particular. Lurking, admittedly rather deep beneath this optimistic surface, however, are elements of a much less cheerful view of spying and of its social implications. For espionage, it turns out on occasion, can be a dirty business which compromises a nation's morality, eats away at a spy's identity, and denies human dignity to innocent bystanders.

The darker face of spying reveals itself most clearly in the personalities of enemy agents, all of whom have suffered a loss of both integrity and identity because of the requirement that they work alone, lie, perform roles and exploit others. In many cases this process is so advanced that the spy no longer possesses any fixed centre of self and simply becomes the part he is playing at any particular time. Ivery, in *Mr Standfast,* can change his appearance and personality so completely as to become unrecognizable, even to those who know him and, like the Baron von Holtzman in Hill's *Spies of Wight,* he is described as a 'chameleon'.[22] A person who has so completely sacrificed his own identity can hardly be expected to have any respect for the uniqueness of his fellow human beings, and the enemy agent is generally ruthless in his dealings with

[22] John Buchan, *Mr Standfast* (Harmondsworth: Penguin, 1956), p. 171; Headon Hill, *Spies of the Wight* (London: Arthur Pearson, 1899), p. 18.

others. Myra Campion's attitude is typical: 'In these international affairs one cannot, unfortunately, regard private feelings.'[23]

In the world of Buchan or Hill despicable behaviour is, of course, what one would expect from any foreigner. However, that we are intended to see a connection between the specific type of corruption manifested in the enemy secret agent and the profession in which he is engaged is made evident by the examination of the way in which British spies are treated by a number of the writers under consideration. Prior to becoming spies, the heroes of popular spy novels are uniformly decent, moral and socially responsible people. A few, William Le Queux's Duckworth Drew and Hugh Morrice, for example, are men made lonely by the loss of love,[24] and they take up a career in espionage because of the opportunities it provides for total isolation. Most, however, have no temperamental leanings whatsoever towards the secret world and rarely enter it by choice. Hannay in *The Thirty-Nine Steps* and Courage in Oppenheim's *the Secret* are both caught up in spying by accident, and Hannay returns to espionage in *Mr Standfast* only because he is ordered to do so.[25] Others, such as Drummond in *Bulldog Drummond* and Carruthers in *The Riddle of the Sands* stumble into espionage activities as a consequence of a more general search for adventure.[26]

Because they lack any predeliction towards the seamier

---

[23] Hill, *Spies of the Wight*, p. 215.

[24] Le Queux, *Revelations of the Secret Service* (London: F. V. White, 1911), p. 26; *Secrets of the Foreign Office* (London: Hutchinson, 1903), p. 190.

[25] John Buchan, *The Thirty-Nine Steps*, in *The Four Adventures of Richard Hannay* (London: Hodder and Stoughton, 1930), pp. 16–18; E. Phillips Oppenheim, *The Secret* (London: Ward, Lock, 1937), p. 23; Buchan, *Mr Standfast*, p. 14.

[26] Cyril MacNeile ('Sapper'), *Bulldog Drummond* (London: Hodder and Stoughton, 1920), pp. 25–8; Erskine Childers, *The Riddle of the Sands* (London: Nelson, n.d.), pp. 17–23.

kinds of activities permitted by spying, British agents typically attempt to impose their gentlemanly codes on espionage. Drummond, for instance, will not attack a man from behind; Jardine, in *The Man from Downing Street,* is still able to feel at the end of his case that he has 'played the game honestly and fairly'; and Davies in *The Riddle of the Sands* insists that, even in espionage, telling the truth can be effective.[27] Nevertheless, spying often requires of them that they act in ways other than they would wish. Drummond is forced to lie; Cheshire, in Oppenheim's *The Spymaster,* has to pretend that he loves Deborah Florestan in order to extract information from her; and Hannay is unable to defeat Ivery except by taking advantage of the human weakness he reveals by loving Mary Lamington.[28]

Thus, for all their innate decency and attempts to function ethically, most British agents experience some degree of moral corruption as a result of their secret activities. Only a few, such as Jardine, who points out that a spy loses the ability to feel, and Cheshire, who comes to the conclusion that 'a spy has no conscience' and ceases 'to exist as a human being' are able to define the nature of the damage that they are causing themselves.[29] However, most are conscious of being somehow soiled by the role of secret agent. It upsets Drummond to lie, even though he does it 'for the state'; Morrice is ashamed to be called 'that dirty word – a spy'; and Drew struggles rather desperately to

[27] MacNeile, *Bulldog Drummond*, p. 99; William Le Queux, *The Man from Downing Street* (London: Hurst and Blackett, 1904), p. 278; Childers, *The Riddle of the Sands*, p. 295.
[28] Cyril MacNeile ('Sapper'), *The Final Count*, in *Bulldog Drummond: His Four Rounds with Carl Peterson* (London: Hodder and Stoughton, 1929), p. 806; E. Phillips Oppenheim, *The Spymaster* (London: Hodder and Stoughton, 1938), p. 131; Buchan, *Mr Standfast*, p. 220.
[29] Le Queux, *The Man from Downing Street*, p. 6; Oppenheim, *The Spymaster*, pp. 131, 129.

distance himself from his espionage role: 'I am an English-man, despite the fact that I am a spy.'[30]

Moral compromise is not the only price that the hero of the early British spy novel pays for involvement in espionage; the isolation experienced while working in the field can cause him to lose personal equilibrium and the need to operate under cover can undermine his sense of self. John Buchan is particularly alert to the problems of isolation, and in *Thirty-Nine Steps* he presents a psychologically astute portrait of the way in which Richard Hannay, pursued on the one side by the Black Stone and on the other by the police, finds it increasingly difficult to sustain the burden of struggling alone across the Scottish High-lands, with the result that at times his self-confidence drains away entirely, leaving him virtually paralysed and helpless.[31] Another of Buchan's heroes, Leithen in *The Powerhouse,* learns that to be effectively isolated, even though surrounded by the crowds of London, can produce overwhelming terror.[32]

Buchan's novels are also the source of a very precise analysis of the consequences of role-playing. He begins by emphasizing, in terms later echoed by le Carré, how completely the agent must become his assumed identity if he is to practice successful deceit. It is not enough to wear different clothes or to alter your appearance; you must also convince yourself you are your part and cultivate the appropriate atmosphere.[33] Ultimately, as Hannay dis-covers in *Mr Standfast,* the repetition of such a process can

---

[30] MacNeile, *The Final Count,* p. 806; Le Queux, *Revelations of the Secret Service,* p. 166; Le Queux, *Secrets of the Foreign Office,* p. 141.
[31] John Buchan, *The Thirty-Nine Steps,* p. 31.
[32] John Buchan, *The Powerhouse* (Edinburgh: Blackwood, 1916), p. 194.
[33] Buchan, *The Thirty-Nine Steps,* pp. 57, 119. For similar terminology in le Carré's works, see *The Honourable Schoolboy,* 'Cover is who you are' (VI, 128).

leave the agent feeling deeply alienated and uncertain of where he belongs in the world: 'I had had three names in two days, and as many characters. I felt as if I had no home or position anywhere, and was only a stray dog with everybody's hand and foot against me. It was an ugly sensation.'[34] Courage, in Oppenheim's *The Secret,* experiences an equally profound loss of identity after taking on the part of 'the head-waiter at the Café Suisse': 'To tell you the truth, Adele, I am a different man now from what I was a half an hour ago. I had forgotten that I was still a living being, and that the world was, after all, a beautiful place. I think I had forgotten that there was such a person as Hardcross Courage.'[35]

In addition to their wide-ranging analysis of the effects of spying on the personality, early espionage novels occasionally raise broader questions about the consequences, for a nation's morality, of employing spies. France and Germany are, for example, judged on a number of occasions to have compromised their ethical positions as a result of their involvement in espionage. Thus, in *England's Peril,* a French diplomat condemns France because its extensive use of 'the system of espionage' deviates from 'the principles of fairness'.[36]

By pulling together isolated incidents and references from a number of novels, I have, of course, given far greater prominence to the darker strains present within early spy novels than they are afforded by the novels themselves. The foreigner's personality may be destroyed by entanglement in espionage but, despite moments of self-disgust, existential terror and loss of identity, the British gentleman spy remains at the end of his adventures the

[34] John Buchan, *Mr Standfast,* p. 140.
[35] E. Phillips Oppenheim, *The Secret,* p. 106.
[36] William Le Queux, *England's Peril* (London: George Newnes, 1900), p. 42.

same decent, unreflective and untroubled person he was at the beginning. Similarly, although France and Germany may have become tainted as a consequence of employing secret agents, no such possibility is allowed in the case of Britain. For Jardine, in *The Man from Downing Street,* Britain is free from the danger of corruption because it spies only in reaction to the secret activities of its enemies and for Bulldog Drummond because, as the only nation fit to be dominant, it is justified in using any tactics, including undercover work, needed to ensure that it retains power.[37]

Since they are concerned primarily to offer mythic affirmations of the worth of British society, it obviously does not suit the purpose of writers such as Buchan, Le Queux or Oppenheim to develop the full implications of their perception that spying is not just a source of heroic adventures but an activity that devalues the individual, denies validity to the emotions, demands of those involved in it that they lie, cheat and assume false identities, and undermines a nation's morality. As a result a number of important themes exist only in embryo, and almost no effort is made to reconcile them with the optimistic vision that lies at the centre of these novels. Buchan, for example, does not seem to feel that there is any need to explain why Hannay emerges whole from adventures, in the course of which he experiences intense isolation, suffers a frequent loss of identity, and is repeatedly forced to offend against the Christian ethics to which he is pledged.

In that they fail to develop the darker aspects of the world that they create the works of the early popular spy novelists possess potential rather than actual complexity. Nevertheless, even by suggesting that espionage fiction can be a vehicle for exploring themes of alienation,

---

[37] Le Queux, *The Man from Downing Street,* p. 5; MacNeile, *The Final Count,* p. 774.

dehumanization, and social decadence as well as for mythopoeic celebrations of social harmony, they afford a completer
sense of the potential of the genre than do the otherwise
more accomplished works of Conrad and Greene. There is
no evidence that le Carré recognized this, and even if he
did, his debt to Conrad and Greene for the techniques
needed to develop the realistic dimensions of the spy novel
is in no way lessened. Yet, given his profound understanding of the development of the British spy novel, it would be
a mistake to dismiss this possibility. And if a direct
influence can indeed be accepted, we are left with the very
satisfying sense that, at the moment it reaches the apex of
accomplishment in the novels of le Carré, the spy novel has
in a very real way returned to its origins.

Le Carré is clearly a spy novelist *par excellence*. The
entire tradition, ranging from the nearly unreadable pot-
boilers of Headon Hill to classics such as *The Secret Agent*
and *The Quiet American,* are grist to his mill and, building
on the very different achievements of his predecessors, he
has demonstrated how a popular genre can be made into a
form sufficiently flexible to accommodate simultaneously a
rigorous critique of modern society and the creation of an
ideal mythic framework. Far from hindering le Carré's
ambitions to become a major writer, his decision to work
largely within the spy novel format was undoubtedly the
single most important factor in bringing them to realization.

# CHAPTER FOUR

# The Recurring George Smiley

THERE CAN BE little doubt that *Smiley's People* brings to an end the cycle of George Smiley novels. Karla has been defeated at last and Smiley, now at least sixty-four, has his thoughts fixed on death rather than future secret enterprises. Although he is unwilling to repeat Conan Doyle's error by pushing Smiley off the Reichenbach Falls, le Carré has more or less admitted that he has no intention of resurrecting his 'anchor man and familiar'[1] of seven novels.[2] In an interview with Tony Chiu he comments, 'I have rounded off the character. Certainly he cannot progress'[3] and he has told a reporter from *Maclean's* that, after *Smiley's People*, 'I had had enough of Smiley.'[4] Le Carré's career is therefore now at a point when it would be appropriate to review some of the questions raised by Smiley's recurring role in his novels.

That le Carré should have found a major part for Smiley in five of his works (*Call for the Dead*, *A Murder of Quality*, *Tinker, Tailor, Soldier, Spy*, *The Honourable Schoolboy*, and *Smiley's People*) and a minor but significant

---

[1] Arthur Hopcraft, 'How Smiley Came to Life', *Telegraph Sunday Magazine*, 21 Oct. 1977, p. 108.

[2] Miriam Gross, 'The Secret World of John le Carré', *Observer*, 13 Nov. 1977, p. 35.

[3] 'Behind the Best Sellers: John le Carré', *New York Times Book Review*, 6 Jan. 1980, p. 30.

[4] Mark Abley, 'John le Carré's Trail of Terror', *Publisher's Weekly* 212, 19 Sept. 1977, p. 48.

one in two others (*The Looking-Glass War* and *The Spy Who Came in from the Cold*) is not at all surprising. So many of the central thematic concerns of le Carré's novels are embodied in the character's commitment to reconciling the rational and feeling aspects of the personality and in his constant questioning of social institutions, that it is little wonder that he so often commands a place at their centre. Furthermore, because of his magisterial intelligence, Smiley has often provided le Carré with a ready solution to the problems inherent in guiding the reader through his complex plots: 'One of the functions of Smiley is to act as a central intellect in whom the reader has so much confidence that when Smiley is becoming analytical and intuitive about things, you more or less leave the reasoning to him.'[5] However, the large proportions that Smiley has finally assumed within le Carré's *oeuvre* have been the result of rather more than a series of individual decisions to return to the same character. The evidence offered both by the novels and the author is that, even as he wrote *Call for the Dead,* le Carré was planning that Smiley's role should be a recurring one. Despite some uncertainty at times about the way in which the character might best be employed and an apparent loss of interest in him after *A Murder of Quality,* some of le Carré's major literary efforts have since been dedicated to developing this role.

Exactly how le Carré has intended Smiley to function throughout his repeated appearances is the first of the topics that the present chapter will address. The author's own recent comments on the subject, the manner in which he presents his hero in *Smiley's People* and the fact that the

[5] Andrew Rutherford, 'Spymaster', *Kaleidoscope*, BBC Radio 4, 13 Sept. 1979, transcript, pp. 5–6.

Smiley novels were published in strict chronological order all suggest that Smiley should be regarded as a developing character. However, as I will demonstrate in detail later, there is really very little evidence to support this argument. Despite continual shifts in his degree of institutional loyalty, which culminate in *Smiley's People* with the total rejection of marriage, the Circus and Britain, Smiley changes very little from first appearance to last. To read all the works in which he appears is therefore to experience a pattern of repetition rather than change, and I will argue that it is within this repetition that the key to le Carré's intentions regarding his central character is to be found.

While the first part of my argument will be directed towards demonstrating the essential fixedness of le Carré's conception of George Smiley, the second will suggest that there is a considerable evolution in his ability to realize this conception. Smiley's role in the novels is a complex one because he is intended to function simultaneously as a fallible human being and as an ideal. In the early stages of his literary career, le Carré lacks the technical resources necessary to give complete fictional life to a character postulated in such paradoxical terms. However, by the time he comes to write *Tinker, Tailor, Soldier, Spy* and *The Honourable Schoolboy,* le Carré is a much more sophisticated artist and is able to create a portrait of Smiley that is at once convincing in its delineation of him as engaged in an endless struggle to come to terms with a world he finds confusing and disturbing and yet establishes him quite firmly as a figure of heroic, and even legendary, proportions. By focusing on their increasingly flexible use of third-person narrative and of the formulas of detective fiction, this chapter will trace the process by which le Carré's novels yield up ever more satisfying versions of George Smiley.

125

# I

The possibility that Smiley might have a recurring role to play in his fiction seems to have been in le Carré's mind as early as the character's first appearance in *Call for the Dead*. The novel opens with a lengthy biographical sketch, entitled somewhat portentously, 'A Brief History of George Smiley', which includes rather more information, particularly about his relationship with Ann, than would be strictly necessary if this were to be Smiley's only fictional appearance. Its ending, in which Smiley is left literally in mid-air on his way to a possible reunion with Ann, also leads the reader to anticipate further encounters with him. However, at this stage of his career, le Carré does not seem to have worked out completely what he might do with Smiley. After trying him out as an amateur detective in *A Murder of Quality*, le Carré returns to the potentially more fertile ground of the spy novel, and even to the world of the Circus, but seems unable to come up with any major parts for Smiley to play. In the course of four novels, *The Spy Who Came in from the Cold*, *The Looking-Glass War*, *A Small Town in Germany*, and *The Naive and Sentimental Lover*, the last of which constitutes a further excursion beyond the boundaries of espionage, Smiley appears only twice, and then only peripherally.

Le Carré seems finally to have come to terms with Smiley at some time during the writing of *Tinker, Tailor, Soldier, Spy*. According to the author's own account of the composition of this novel, Smiley was again absent from the first draft and found his way in initially because 'he is ... very consoling to have around in a complex plot.'[6]

---

[6] Gross, 'The Secret World of John le Carré', p. 35.

Once included, however, Smiley at last took a firm grip on his creator's imagination, and le Carré went to some lengths in his rewriting of *Tinker, Tailor, Soldier, Spy* to establish him as the focal point of his fictional world. First le Carré reiterates a number of details from the description and biography offered in *Call for the Dead* in order to create a continuity with the Smiley of the earlier novels. Thus, reference is made to Smiley's expensive but ill-fitting clothes (*CD*, I, 9; *TT*, II, 23); there is an allusion to his war-time field service in Germany (*CD*, I, 13; *TT*, XXI, 272); and his house is located in Bywater Street (*CD*, V, 45; *TT*, III, 31). The reappearance of Smiley's friend Mendel, the retired policeman, who, as he did in the earlier novel, lives in a semi-detached house in Mitcham and keeps bees (*CD*, V, 38; VI, 47; *TT*, XXV, 213) establishes a further link between the worlds of *Call for the Dead* and *Tinker, Tailor, Soldier, Spy*.

Second, as preparation for future appearances, le Carré alters Smiley's biography in several respects. The date at which Smiley graduated from Oxford is revised from 1928 (*CD*, I, 10) to 1937 (*TT*, XII, 97; XXIX, 250), thereby reducing his age by nine years and making more plausible the continuation of his intelligence activities into the late 1970s. A meeting with Karla is introduced into Smiley's past in order to account for the intensity of the running battle in which they are to be engaged until the end of *Smiley's People*. To accommodate this encounter, le Carré offers a revised version of Smiley's role during the 1950s. Whereas in *Call for the Dead* his career had ground to a desk-bound halt by this time, in *Tinker, Tailor, Soldier, Spy* he is presented as travelling the world to arrange the defection of Russian agents. One of these is a certain Gerstmann, who, of course, turns out to be Karla (*CD*, I, 15; *TT*, XXIII, 194). And finally, the time during which the Circus operates under Maston's leadership becomes in

*Tinker, Tailor, Soldier, Spy* a 'short' (XVI, 129) one rather than, as is suggested in *Call for the Dead* and *The Spy Who Came in from the Cold,* lasting from just after the war until the end of the Fennan case in 1960. This change allows Control to take over as head of the Circus in the late 1940s and thereby adds the kind of longevity to their relationship needed to explain the depth of feeling with which Smiley reacts in *Tinker, Tailor, Soldier, Spy* and *The Honourable Schoolboy* to Karla's betrayal of Control.

These revisions in Smiley's biography lend considerable credence to le Carré's claim that, even as he wrote *Tinker, Tailor, Soldier, Spy,* he was planning the trilogy of novels now called *The Quest for Karla,*[7] and it is not surprising that there is an almost complete coherence in the presentation of the final years of his hero's career as an agent. *The Honourable Schoolboy* picks up the history of the Circus some six months after the death of Bill Haydon, and *Smiley's People* begins three years after Smiley's enforced retirement from the Circus at the termination of Operation Dolphin. The chronological relationship between these novels is so carefully worked out that a key event in *The Honourable Schoolboy,* Smiley's trip to Hong Kong in April 1975, is used in *Smiley's People* as an explanation for the failure of Vladimir's earlier attempts to move against Karla (*SP,* XI, 176).

The history of le Carré's use of George Smiley is obviously rather a complicated one. Nevertheless, two important points emerge with some clarity. First, except for a rather striking loss of direction between the publication of *A Murder of Quality* and the final stages in the composition of *Tinker, Tailor, Soldier, Spy,* it has been in

---

[7] Rutherford, 'Spymaster', p. 5. According to le Carré's agent, George Greenfield, the series was originally intended to run to six novels. This information is provided in a letter to the author, dated 16 August 1984.

le Carré's mind throughout his career that Smiley should play a recurring role in his fiction. Second, in restoring Smiley to centre stage in *Tinker, Tailor, Soldier, Spy* and in preparing the way for his use in the other two parts of a proposed trilogy, le Carré strives to establish as much continuity as possible with earlier versions of the character. It seems reasonable, therefore, to regard the seven manifestations of George Smiley as the product of a single, consistent imaginative impulse.

## II

In recent years, le Carré has suggested several times that a reading of the Smiley novels will reveal him to be a developing character. On one occasion he comments that 'He and I have grown up a lot since the first book.'[8] On another that 'The Smiley of the first book was not the Smiley of *Tinker, Tailor*. *Tinker, Tailor* was written seventeen years later and by that time both Smiley and I were seeing the world in a rather different way.'[9] And on still another: 'I think Smiley changes very much from book to book.'[10] In order to be in a position to consider the merits of these claims we must have a firm grasp on the basic components of the character's personality and situation, as defined at the time of his first and chronologically earliest fictional appearance in *Call for the Dead*.

Smiley's purpose is the achievement of a full and complex humanity which, so far as he is concerned, involves a reconciliation of the rational and emotional (or sentimental and naive) aspects of his personality. The problem

[8] Chiu, 'Behind the Best Sellers', p. 30.
[9] Arthur Hopcraft, 'How Smiley Came to Life', p. 108.
[10] Rutherford, 'Spymaster', p. 6.

for Smiley is that much of his experience is heavily polarized. As a scholar and in his career as a spy he must often be 'bloodless and inhuman' (I, 12) and take his pleasure from 'academic excursions into the mystery of human behaviour, disciplined by the practical application of his own deductions' (I, 10). As Ann's lover, on the other hand, he is completely at the mercy of his feelings. However, far as he might be from achieving what he later calls his ideal of 'moderation' (*TT*, XXIII, 207) or 'a reasonable balance in human affairs' (*HS*, V, 118), Smiley is at least clear as to the kind of relationship that should exist between 'humanity' and 'reason' (*SP*, XII, 136). For him, experience begins properly in the present moment and in the individual's emotional response to that moment. This is the 'habit of reality' which Ann taught him when she made 'the present so important' (*CD*, V, 37–8). However, unlike Ann, Smiley does not consider the feeling response to be enough because, in his view, the individual must function coherently through time and not just spasmodically in a series of intense moments. For this goal to be achieved, feelings must be analysed and the significant truths thereby uncovered, used as the basis for general principles of thought and behaviour. Smiley's code of concern for others and his creed of service derives quite directly, for example, from the most important of all the emotional responses, the impulse to care for or to love another person. By contrast the same impulse simply leads Ann into a series of affairs.

Smiley is acutely aware that, left to his own resources, the individual is likely to make only limited progress in a quest for wholeness of personality. Therefore, he seeks to affiliate himself with a society whose customs and institutions offer a model of how the person's desire for order and pattern can be balanced against the needs of spontaneous individuality. During his early adulthood, Smiley judged Britain worthy of his allegiance, especially when compared to a fascist Germany which denied any value to the products of the individual spirit, as evidenced in the book-burnings he witnessed in 1937. He looks to two of the society's institutions in particular, the Secret Service and marriage, to provide him with the kind of context he is seeking. The Circus in initially attractive to Smiley, partly because its function is to protect British society against the threats posed by countries like Germany and partly because it operates in a spirit of 'inspired amateurism' (I, 14) that seems thoroughly coherent with the individualistic values it is defending. He is drawn to marriage because it offers the obvious institutional haven within which to foster love, which he has discovered is the most profound of all human emotions.

However, by 1960, when the events of *Call for the Dead* take place Smiley has begun to have serious doubts about the value of Britain, the Circus and marriage. The problem, so far as he is concerned, with Britain and the Circus is that both have become so deeply penetrated by 'efficiency, bureaucracy and intrigue' (I, 14) that an imbalance has developed between the claims of the group and those of the individual. A distaste for the new communist enemy, characterized by 'the fabulous impertinence of renouncing the individual in favour of the mass' and which makes use of 'blank, soulless automatons like Mundt' to further its goal, 'to shape the world as if it were a tree, cutting off what did not fit the regular image' (XVI, 126) is finally strong enough to convince Smiley that he should remain loyal to Britain. However, he turns away from the Circus because he considers that, under Maston's leadership, the smooth functioning of administrative machinery has become such a primary concern that it no longer exercises any useful function. Therefore, while Smiley continues to struggle throughout *Call for the Dead* to counter communist assaults on British society, he does so in a private capacity.

The value of marriage is much less evident to Smiley in 1959 than it became towards the end of the war, because of the almost total failure of the institution to accommodate his relationship with Ann. For Ann 'holy matrimony' (I, 10) provides an appropriate demonstration of her love for Smiley, but she will not agree to be bound by its monogomous conventions. Therefore, she begins her first affair only two years after their wedding and is apart from Smiley throughout the Fennan case. Elsa Fennan's willingness to make her marital obligations subservient to communist ideology, and ultimately to collude in her husband's murder, further points up for Smiley the inadequacies of the institution. However, even though his and others' experience may have eroded Smiley's faith, he is not yet willing to reject marriage, and as *Call for the Dead* ends, so he is setting out to attempt yet another reunion with Ann.

The other important aspect of Smiley's situation explored in *Call for the Dead* involves his attitude to the ethics of espionage. Smiley becomes a spy out of a concern for individual freedom, and yet he finds that the methods of his chosen profession involve that very exploitation of the individual which it is his goal to prevent. The painful conflict between ends and means which results, and the emotional and moral turmoil into which it throws Smiley, are sharply illustrated by his conduct of the Fennan case. To save Britain from the threat posed by the absolutist ideology of Elsa Fennan and Dieter Frey, Smiley manipulates their lives in such a way that they are both eventually killed and thereby deprives them very finally of their individual freedom. Smiley's awareness of the implications of his behaviour is demonstrated by the acute despair he experiences at the moment of supposed triumph: 'Dieter was dead, and he had killed him. The broken fingers of his right hand, the stiffness of his body and the sickening headache, the nausea of guilt, all testified to this' (XVI, 133).

Although le Carré has been fairly consistent in arguing that later versions of Smiley differ significantly from the one that appears in *Call for the Dead,* only twice, in interviews with Melvyn Bragg and Mark Abley, does he offer any clue to the kind of changes that are supposed to have taken place. He states to Bragg: 'By the end of the Smiley books I'd gone too far into a private world.'[11] That Smiley himself bears the burden of this shift is made clear in a comment le Carré offers to Abley: 'I had had enough of Smiley [by the end of *Smiley's People*] ... His profound disenchantment with the world seemed to be, at times, an excuse for not engaging in it.'[12] The nature of this disenchantment is defined quite precisely in *Smiley's People* where le Carré argues that a lifetime experience of 'English muddle' (XII, 136) and, more specifically, the betrayal of Britain and the Circus by Bill Haydon, a member of the inner circle of both, have caused Smiley to lose faith in the society and the major institution which he has served throughout his adult life. Ann's ultimate betrayal in taking as her lover Bill Haydon, who is friend, colleague and set, has been the cause, it is suggested, of an equally firm rejection of marriage. His change in perspective is defined thus:

> Even five years ago he would never have admitted to such sentiments. But today, peering calmly into his

---

[11] 'A Talk with John le Carré', *New York Times Book Review,* 13 March 1983, p. 22. Leroy L. Panek offers a similar interpretation in 'John le Carré', *The Special Branch* (Bowling Green: Bowling Green University Popular Press, 1981), p. 247.
[12] Abley, 'John le Carré's Trail of Terror'. p. 48.

own heart, Smiley knew that he was unled, and perhaps unleadable; that the only restraints upon him were those of his own reason, and his own humanity. As with his marriage, so with his sense of public service. I invested my life in institutions – he thought without rancour – and all I am left with is myself. (XII, 136)

Smiley's movement inwards is completed, according to le Carré, by the narrowing of his antipathy to communism into a personal vendetta against Karla, the man who shattered his 'last illusions' (XII, 137) by directing Haydon to seduce Ann. This is made evident by Smiley's complete disregard for the enormous intelligence benefits which will accrue to Britain if Karla can be persuaded to defect. So far as he is concerned the mission is no more than a 'lonely quest' (XII, 128) and the only motives he will acknowledge are revenge and a desire for personal 'resolution' (XXIII, 266).

Thus, the argument advanced generally by le Carré in the Chiu, *Telegraph Sunday Magazine* and Rutherford interviews, and more specifically in the Bragg and Abley interviews and in *Smiley's People* is that the various fictional manifestations of Smiley trace a long pattern of evolution which, broadly speaking, involves a sloughing off of institutional loyalties and a withdrawal into 'a private world'. However, two flaws are immediately apparent in the very cornerstone of the analysis of Smiley's development offered in *Smiley's People*. First, even if this analysis is accepted, significant changes in Smiley would appear to derive entirely from his experience of Bill Haydon in *Tinker, Tailor, Soldier, Spy*. Therefore, it sharply contradicts the suggestion made by le Carré in the *Telegraph Sunday Magazine* that Smiley's way of viewing the world had already evolved significantly during the seventeen years following the writing of *Call for the Dead*. Second, and still more important, based on a close reading of what actually happens in those novels, there seems good reason to doubt a major part of the argument made in *Smiley's People* about the ways in which Smiley changes during the *Quest for Karla* trilogy.

Le Carré appears to be on firm ground only when he argues that Smiley's final alienation from Ann and from marriage has its roots in her affair with Bill Haydon. *Tinker, Tailor, Soldier, Spy* ends, like *Call for the Dead*, with Smiley involved in yet another attempt to revive his flagging marriage. On this occasion, however, his efforts seem bound to fail, for even as he first catches sight of Ann, he recognizes that she is 'essentially another man's woman' (XXXVIII, 348). This image becomes so firmly planted in Smiley's mind that, although he lives with Ann again for a short time at the beginning of *The Honourable Schoolboy*, he soon takes the unprecedented step of abandoning her. By the end of the novel their alienation is alleviated only by occasional lunches and Smiley shows no signs of responding to Ann's desire for a reconciliation. The three years that intervene between *The Honourable Schoolboy* and *Smiley's People* simply harden this situation. The affair with Haydon still dominates Smiley's thinking about Ann: ' "It's to do with the people who ruined Bill Haydon," he said to her. . . . But he thought: "Who ruined you" ' (XX, 252). Therefore he continues to ignore her requests 'to be together again' (XII, 128), and a relationship which has dwindled away over the course of three novels surely reaches its end with Smiley's assertion that 'he belonged nowhere near her . . . she was like a girl on a floating island that was swiftly moving away from him with the shadows of all her lovers gathered round her' (XX, 251).

It is not possible, however, to find the same kind of clear connection between Smiley's rejection of the Circus and of

Britain in *Smiley's People* and the events of 'five years ago' (XII, 136). Indeed, far from beginning to turn him away from institutional loyalties, the immediate effect of the Haydon scandal is to increase Smiley's commitment to country and Secret Service. Thus, national loyalties expressed elliptically in *Call for the Dead* as part of Smiley's rejection of communism, or grudgingly in *Tinker, Tailor, Soldier, Spy* where he professes only to prefer his role as a 'flabby Western liberal' (XXIII, 205) to that of the absolutist Karla, are asserted with considerable conviction in *The Honourable Schoolboy*. When Smiley rebuffs Westerby for allowing his affair with Lizzie Worthington to endanger Operation Dolphin, he has, for example, no hesitation in identifying himself with Britain as 'we': 'Jerry, you don't understand what's going on. How much you could upset things. Billions of dollars and thousands of men could not obtain a part of what we stand to gain from this one operation' (XX, 482).

Similarly, Smiley has never previously worked in such close accord with the Circus as he does in *The Honourable Schoolboy*. His usual position is at the edge of the secret world; he actually resigns from the Circus in *Call for the Dead*, is officially retired in *The Spy Who Came in from the Cold* and carries out his undercover work under cover in *Tinker, Tailor, Soldier, Spy*. In *The Honourable Schoolboy*, however, Smiley has become head of the Circus. As such, his role is a much more active one than ever before. Instead of simply responding to the aggressive acts of the enemy or participating in Control's schemes, Smiley begins to seek out opportunities for mounting intelligence operations. Smiley's relationship to the Circus is also different in that he now functions as part of a large team which includes Connie, de Salis, Guillam, Craw, Westerby, Molly Meakin and others, rather than as an isolated and lonely seeker whose efforts are occasionally supported by a small band of select friends.

Implicit in Smiley's altered position within the structure of the Circus is an intensification of his institutional commitment which manifests itself most obviously in his attitude to the mission at hand. Usually, the deeper Smiley is drawn into a case, the more he is torn between his final goal and his sense of responsibility for the individuals he must exploit to achieve this goal. Consequently, his typical mood, particularly as things draw to a conclusion, is one of acute anxiety. The unravelling of the puzzles set by Operation Dolphin, however, often produces in Smiley a most uncharacteristic joviality. His success in connecting Ko to Ricardo's China enterprise inspires, for example, 'a rare fit of excitement' and he even goes so far as to tease Guillam: 'Don't you *understand*, Peter? . . . Oh, you are a dunce!' (XII, 280).

This lightening of Smiley's demeanour is directly related to a narrowing and simplifying in his area of moral concern. The Circus and its objectives are now of paramount importance to him, and even though he is still capable of mourning his dead agents (III, 61), Smiley is willing, to quite a significant extent, to discount the claims of the individual and to overlook discrepancies between ends and means. This is evident not only in his confident rejection of Westerby's attempts to establish parity between his obligations to Lizzie Worthington and to the Circus, but also in his ability to accept the hideous death of Frost because 'operationally, nothing is amiss' (XIV, 324). Smiley's acknowledgement that the successful conclusion of the case merits the sacrifice of his old friend, Westerby, provides a still more telling example of his new attitude.

In *The Honourable Schoolboy*, Smiley identifies so completely with the Circus and the ethos of espionage that he expects nothing but betrayal even for himself. The unscrupulous tactics employed by Sam Collins to reestablish his place in the Circus arouse no resentment in Smiley: 'We are not above a little blackmail ourselves from time to time . . . and it is perfectly reasonable that we should have to submit to it occasionally' (XI, 240). His reaction to the conspiracy which removes him from his position as head of the Circus is equally complaisant: '*These people terrify me but I am one of them. If they stab me in the back, then at least that is the judgment of my peers*' (XXII, 532).

Smiley's attitude to institutions, except for marriage, the rejection of which can clearly be traced back to Ann's affair with Haydon, thus goes through a series of radical shifts in *Tinker, Tailor, Soldier, Spy, The Honourable Schoolboy* and *Smiley's People* rather than following, as le Carré argues, any coherent pattern of development. Recognition of this undercuts not only le Carré's claims about Smiley's role in these last novels, but also his broader contention that there are significant differences between these later versions of the character and earlier ones. The Smiley who struggles desperately between 1973 and 1978 to place himself within institutional contexts only to draw back from them in horror when they fail to meet his individual needs is completely congruent with the Smiley of *Call for the Dead* and the novels which follow it. Thus, he is separated from and reunited with Ann in *Call for the Dead* and separated from her again in *A Murder of Quality*; he rejects the Circus in *Call for the Dead* and yet is meticulous in carrying out Control's orders in *The Spy Who Came in from the Cold* and *The Looking-Glass War*; and he seriously questions his allegiance to Britain in both *Call for the Dead* and *A Murder of Quality*, in which he is deeply critical of a ruling class educated at bastions of reaction and snobbery such as Carne, but serves the national cause loyally throughout the difficult and dangerous investigation into Samuel Fennan's death and the distasteful sequence of deceptions which he is forced to perpetrate in *The Spy Who Came in from the Cold*.

There would seem to be little merit in le Carré's suggestion that a coherent pattern of development underlies Smiley's relationship to institutions. Nevertheless, his constant questioning and periodic rejection of individual institutions does eventually coalesce in *Smiley's People* into a total alienation from all three of his major institutional affiliations. In order to deal completely with the thesis advanced by le Carré we must consider, therefore, whether this final drastic shift in situation is accompanied by the profound change in personality which he defines as having 'gone too far into a private world'. What le Carré appears to mean by this is that, in cutting himself free from institutions, Smiley has lost all connection with the world outside. Since the most basic of the naive impulses that have been so important to Smiley's concept of self is that which directs him to care for others, implicit within a change of attitude of this kind is a complete yielding of his search for full humanity.

At the core of le Carré's argument that his hero is different in *Smiley's People* is the contention that, having been stripped of its social and ideological dimensions, Smiley's quest for Karla is now nothing more than an acting out of personal obsessions. This very possibility does in fact occur to Smiley himself several times in earlier novels: 'he did honestly wonder whether Ann was right, and his striving had become nothing other than a private journey among the beasts and villains of his own insufficiency' (*HS*, XXI, 499). That he should have experienced such moments of self-doubt is inevitable because – and to understand this is essential to obtaining a clear view of Smiley's role in *Smiley's People* – his opposition to Karla has always had personal rather than ideological roots. However, prior to *Smiley's People* there has never been any suggestion that there is anything fundamentally wrong with this. Indeed, given the nature of Smiley's approach to experience, it would be odd if he had taken any other approach. Abstractions are anathema to Smiley and so, just as he focuses his energies in *Call for the Dead* into hatred of Frey rather than of communism, so in *Tinker, Tailor, Soldier, Spy* and *The Honourable Schoolboy* he sets himself against Karla rather than Moscow (*HS*, IV, 97).

Our concern, then, must not be so much with the removal from his quest of its national dimension, because this has never been more than secondary, but with that same question that has always preoccupied Smiley: why does he hate Karla? The answer would seem to be, as it always has been, because he is an absolutist who makes individual considerations subservient to the furtherance of larger ideological goals. Smiley is spurred on in *Smiley's People* by discovering, in quick succession, that his old adversary is responsible for the murders of Vladimir and Leipzig and for the attempted murder of Ostrakova, much as he is in *Tinker, Tailor, Soldier, Spy* by ever-increasing knowledge of how Karla has manipulated and misused Prideaux, Ann and Control. The fact that amongst Karla's exploitative acts has been an attack on 'the temples of his private faith' (*HS*, V, 118) sharpens, as it has done in the two previous novels, Smiley's perception of his enemy's nature and adds to his resolve rather than containing his quest within the boundaries of private obsession. Thus, when Smiley takes on Karla he is acting not just for himself, but for Vladimir, Leipzig, Ostrakova and by implication all individuals. That lack of an institutional context within which to function has in no way diminished the intensity of Smiley's human concerns is demonstrated with particular clarity in the anguish he experiences at the realization of how, while struggling in defence of individualism, he has been guilty of exploiting Karla's individuality: 'an unholy vertigo seized him as the very evil he had fought against seemed to reach out and possess him and claim him despite his striving, calling him a traitor also' (*SP*, XXVII, 324). Such a reaction would be beyond the capacity of a man locked within a private world, especially when the object of his concern is also his most implacable enemy.

Far from retreating into the self, Smiley is, if anything, a more deeply caring person during the action of *Smiley's People* than at any other time during his fictional career. Certainly he has transcended a certain scepticism about the claims of feeling which accompanied his disillusionment with Ann in *The Honourable Schoolboy*, and which manifested itself with particular strength during his debate with Westerby about the nature of his obligations to Lizzie Worthington: 'he had not the smallest doubt that at this moment Jerry's feeling for the girl was a cause which Ann would warmly have espoused. But he was not Ann either' (XXI, 499). Thus, in *Smiley's People*, a regard for feeling stands firmly at the centre of Smiley's universe, and he clearly acknowledges the essential part played by love in the process by which the individual achieves complete fulfilment. Far from celebrating the condition of aloneness which he has achieved by his rejection of Ann and of marriage, Smiley judges himself to be incomplete and empathizes deeply with other men, such as Vladimir, who live alone: 'we men who cook for ourselves are half-creatures' (VII, 76) and those such as Lacon and Mikhel, who have been betrayed in love: 'Smiley found himself looking into his own face as he had glimpsed it too often, red-eyed like Mikhel's, in Ann's pretty gilt mirrors in their house in Bywater Street' (X, 115). Lovers such as Villem and Stella and the young couple at Leipzig's house in Hamburg, friends such as Leipzig and Kretzschmar, and caring fathers and daughters such as Karla and Tatiana win his unreserved admiration and affection.

Further evidence of Smiley's orientation away from

141

purely private concerns is provided by his willingness in *Smiley's People* to commit his personal resources, both naive and sentimental, as fully as ever to the task of making a reality out of his humanistic ideals. Thus, Karla is finally defeated, not because Smiley is made of nobler stuff and has finer feelings, important as these factors are in helping him to recognize his enemy, but because he is willing to embroil himself in the world. The Smiley of *Smiley's People* travels much more extensively than in any other novel, and will do anything he deems necessary, ranging from gestures of acute caring, to cajoling, lying, and role playing (the techniques of his old profession) to achieve his goals.

In *Smiley's People*, then, Smiley is, as he ever was, a man of 'goodwill', 'humanity' (XVIII, 221) and of 'passionate caring' (XVIII, 222), completely dedicated to translating his ideals into reality. He has turned away from institutions, as he has often threatened to do in the past, but in no sense does his behaviour lend credence to le Carré's claim that he has become too private, or that his personality has experienced any significant alteration. Principles of continuity rather than change clearly underlie le Carré's conception of George Smiley, as is made very clear by a comparison of his role in this, his last fictional appearance, and in *Call for the Dead*, his first.

In each novel, Smiley's initial impulse to act is provided by an emotional response to the exploitation of a specific individual. Concern for Samuel Fennan, a man he met only briefly but liked, makes him unwilling to accept the official and convenient verdict of death by suicide, and affection for Vladimir, his former colleague, inspires him to probe more deeply into the cause of his death than is allowed for in his mandate to 'pour oil on the waters' (*SP*, V, 63). This same habit of mind is also evident in Smiley's identification of his target as an individual – Dieter Frey in the first instance, Karla in the second – against whom he directs a good deal of personal animus, rather than as an ideology or a nation.

In his conduct of both cases, however, Smiley shows a clear awareness of the limits of feeling as a guide to conduct. In *Call for the Dead*, he chastizes himself as a 'fool of his own sentiment' (XIV, 112) because sympathy for Elsa Fennan has blinded him temporarily to her lies, and in *Smiley's People* he ruthlessly suppresses his horrified reaction to Leipzig's brutal death. In each instance he realizes that only by acting as a pure technician and making full use of his powers of reason can he hope to uncover the truth.

Smiley is also willing, early and late in his career, to accept that when he functions as a technician he will often offend against that very concern for the individual that he is ultimately seeking to defend. Thus, his manipulation of Elsa Fennan and Dieter Frey in *Call for the Dead* is mirrored by his blackmailing of Grigoriev and Karla in *Smiley's People*. On neither occasion, though, does he duck away from the implications of his actions, and his sense of guilt is equally acute in both instances.

Smiley's institutional loyalties are stronger in *Call for the Dead* than in *Smiley's People*. However, it is almost as evident in this early novel as in the late that Smiley is sceptical about the ability of contemporary institutions to provide a suitable framework for his personal quest. His tolerance for the Circus under Maston is no greater than it is under Enderby, and his commitment to Britain and to marriage is maintained in the face of a clear awareness of the declining state of the nation and of his wife's disloyalty.

Why le Carré ever denied that Smiley is intended to be an essentially unchanging character must remain something of a mystery, because, in the novels which precede

*Smiley's People,* he goes to some lengths to discourage a chronological approach to the character. Smiley's appearance, for example, scarcely changes over the course of his long career until, in *Smiley's People,* a slight deafness and extra chins begin to transform him into an old man. Entering middle age early and leaving it late, a process aided by the downward revision of his age in *Tinker, Tailor, Soldier, Spy,* Smiley is very much in 1973 what he was when he married Ann towards the end of the war. At the time of his marriage, he is described thus: 'Short, fat and of a quiet disposition, he appeared to spend a lot of money on really bad clothes, which hung about his squat frame like skin on a shrunken toad' (*CD,* I, 9). And, at the beginning of *Tinker, Tailor, Soldier, Spy* in the following way: 'Small, podgy and at best middle-aged, he was by appearance one of London's meek who do not inherit the earth. His legs were short, his gait anything but agile, his dress costly, ill-fitting and extremely wet' (II, 23). Defined at the beginning of *Call for the Dead* as 'breathtakingly ordinary' (I, 9), Smiley continues throughout his career to be described in the most mundane of terms. His appearance in both *A Murder of Quality,* the action of which takes place in 1960, and in *The Honourable Schoolboy,* some fourteen years later, is that of the typical mediocre office worker: 'he was at first sight the very prototype of an unsuccessful middle-aged bachelor in a sedentary occupation' (*MQ,* II, 165); 'Smiley was acting himself, but more so ... the gentle, decent civil servant who had reached his ceiling by the age of forty, and stayed there ever since' (*HS,* X, 218). Similarly, for both a fellow air passenger in 1960 and for le Carré in 1974, he fits into yet another archetype of mediocrity: the pathetic middle-aged seeker after sexual pleasures: 'The young, fair-haired man beside him examined him closely out of the corner of his eye. He knew the type well – the tired executive out for a bit of fun. He found it rather disgusting' (*CD*, XVIII, 143); 'Smiley walked, one round little man in a raincoat ... the mackintosh brigade personified, cannonfodder of the mixed sauna parlours and the naughty bookshops' (*HS*, V, 117).

The singleness of le Carré's conception of Smiley is further emphasized by the repetition of certain characteristic behavioural tics. The most famous of these is his habit of polishing his glasses on the end of his tie, a gesture which becomes so much a part of him by 1978 as to contribute to his legendary status: 'He gave a studious frown, and blinked, then whipped off his spectacles and, to the secret delight of everyone, unconsciously subscribed to his own legend by polishing them on the fat end of his tie' (*HS*, XII, 282).

The effect of le Carré's descriptive method is to direct the reader towards approaching each manifestation of Smiley as a complete creation rather than as a provisional portrait able to be understood only as part of a sequence of younger and older versions of the character offered in earlier and later novels. Le Carré further encourages this approach by repeating, in the course of every novel in which Smiley plays a central role, the essential biographical information first presented in *Call for the Dead*. Through narrative commentary, Smiley's interior monologue or conversation, the reader is always provided with the crucial details of his early career – his Oxford education, his war-time espionage experience in Germany, and his marriage to and early betrayal by Ann. In *Tinker, Tailor, Soldier, Spy*, for example, the narrator lets the reader know that Smiley was once a student at Oxford: 'There are old men who go back to Oxford and find their youth beckoning to them from the stones. Smiley was not one of them ... Passing the Bodleian he vaguely thought: I worked there' (XXI, 97); Smiley's own thoughts return the action briefly to war-time Germany: 'for a moment Smiley was back in occupied Germany, in his own time as a field agent' (XXXI, 272); and Guillam's memory, picking up on a comment offered by Smiley, makes it clear that Ann was well launched on her career of affairs by 1955: 'Yes, Guillam had heard about that too, a twenty-year-old Welsh Apollo, the season's wonder boy. They had been burning up London for months' (XXIII, 196).

Le Carré's concern to make Smiley's appearances independent of one another is particularly marked during the *Quest for Karla* novels. Conceived as a trilogy, they are certainly much more tightly bound in terms of plot than the earlier Smiley novels. Nevertheless, le Carré makes extensive use of repetition in order to ensure that each can be read in isolation. The details of Ann's affair with Haydon are, for example, reiterated in both *The Honourable Schoolboy* and *Smiley's People* (*HS*, III, 52–3; V, 119; *SP*, XII, 128), as is the account of Smiley's meeting with Karla in India (*HS*, V, 118; *SP*, XII, 136–8).

For most of his career, then, le Carré's intention with respect to George Smiley has been to create again and again the same image of a short, fat, bespectacled, permanently middle-aged and worried little man who struggles with all his resources to make sense of and to gain control over the complex and often contradictory elements out of which both his own personality and his world are composed. Far from revealing any limitations in le Carré's creative powers, as perhaps he has begun to suspect himself, if his recent revisionist exercises are any indication, it is the very fixedness of the author's conception of Smiley that gives the character its special force. Le Carré clearly points up the role he wishes Smiley to play with the following comment: 'I feel, as I think Smiley does, that the components of life as we live it are irreconcilable and

chaotic. The art of survival is to function in spite of this.'[13]
In such a universe there can never be any resolution and
were Smiley to progress or to find answers, it could only be
because he or his creator had been false to his notion of the
anarchic state of things. Thus, Smiley's ability to commit
himself again and again to the same task of making sense
of the unintelligible and order out of the intrinsically
chaotic marks him out as a model of le Carré's faith in the
resilience of the human spirit and as a man of truly heroic
proportions. A reading of all the Smiley novels will be
more satisfying than a reading of any one of them, not
because it will show the character developing but because
it will enable this pattern of repetition fully to emerge.
Smiley's situation alters markedly from novel to novel. In
*Call for The Dead, A Murder of Quality, Tinker, Tailor,
Soldier, Spy* and *Smiley's People,* for instance, he operates
at the edge or outside of institutions, while in *The Spy
Who Came in from the Cold, The Looking-Glass War,*
and *The Honourable Schoolboy* he functions within terms
defined for him by the Circus. His role is subject to equally
sharp inversions. Thus, whereas Ann's affairs repeatedly
assign Smiley the part of the betrayed, he is in turn the
betrayer of Drake Ko's love for his brother, Nelson, Karla's
affection for his daughter, Tatiana, and Fred Leiser's
dedication to his country. Similarly, he works in *Tinker,
Tailor, Soldier, Spy* to break down Ricki Tarr's intellectual
control by making him feel pain at the possible loss of his
loved ones, but struggles in *Smiley's People* to translate his
own anguish at Vladimir's death into the rational analysis
needed to gain advantage in his battle with Karla. However, the more his situation and role change the more
evident it is that, at root, Smiley remains the same man

---

[13] Gross, 'The Secret World of John le Carré', p. 33.

from novel to novel, and never wavers in his basic commitment to the hopeless but heroic pursuit of what he calls 'resolution' (*SP*, XXIII, 266).

## III

Although le Carré's intentions regarding George Smiley have remained essentially unchanged, we do not, in reading the novels in which he appears, experience the character in precisely the same way. This sense of difference reflects the considerable development which has taken place over the years in le Carré's ability to give fictional shape to his ideas about Smiley. Beginning with Smiley's first appearance in *Call for the Dead*, le Carré has struggled to find techniques appropriate to the presentation of a character conceived in quite paradoxical terms as being like ourselves and an ideal, a person who is better than us because he feels more deeply, thinks more incisively and comes much closer to making sense out of the world around him. In order to understand how, in *Tinker, Tailor, Soldier, Spy* and *The Honourable Schoolboy* and to a lesser extent in *Smiley's People*, le Carré eventually succeeds in the difficult task he has set himself, we must examine in some detail the major shifts in technique that occur as he returns again and again to the same character.

In *Call for the Dead* and *A Murder of Quality*, le Carré employs what Wayne Booth has called a third-person 'centre of consciousness' or 'reflector' narrative technique.[14] Thus, the action of both novels is presented by an external narrator, who limits his potential omniscience so that for much of the time the reader sees the world from

[14] *The Rhetoric of Fiction* (Chicago: University of Chicago Press, 1961), p. 153. Also see pp. 271–398 for detailed discussion of this topic.

the point of view of a single character, George Smiley. Le Carré is not completely rigid in his use of the technique and we do occasionally move away from Smiley. The narrator himself provides a good deal of information and offers many judgements; there are a number of scenes from which Smiley is absent; and occasionally we are given access to the mind of another character. The first chapter of *Call for the Dead,* for example, consists entirely of the narrator's summary and assessment of the life and of the philosophical and social attitudes of his hero, and *A Murder of Quality* begins with the narrator's rather wide-ranging account of the history of Carne School and presentation of two scenes that do not include Smiley – a conversation between two pupils and Fielding's dinner party. Other points of view which are provided from time to time include Mendel's in *Call for the Dead* (X, 76ff) and Ailsa Brimley's in *A Murder of Quality* (II, 168). On the whole, though, Smiley's consciousness dominates and not even the narrator presents an alternative perspective on the action, because his judgements usually coincide with Smiley's. The narrator's assessment of Carne, for example: 'Carne had property, cloisters and woodworm, a whipping block and a line in the Doomsday Book – then what more did it need to instruct the sons of the rich?' (*MQ*, I, 151), is similar in content and cynical tone to that offered by Smiley: 'Staring across the neglected hotel gardens towards Carne Abbey, he was able to glimpse behind the lead roof of the Abbey the familiar battlements of the school: keeping the new world out and the old world secure' (IX, 223).

This technique is effective in that it firmly establishes Smiley's central position within le Carré's fictional world and, by equating his views with those of the narrator, lends him a good deal of authority. Most important of all, however, le Carré is able to provide the reader with an intimate view of the workings of Smiley's deeply reflective, ever-questioning, and always troubled mind. The sequence of thoughts, for example, in which he goes from musing on his failure to derive the solace he once did from driving a car, to the part played by Ann in his loss of peace of mind, and then to his deep sympathy for Elsa Fennan and simultaneous recognition that, as is always the case in human relationships, he does not know her at all, is much more effective in defining Smiley's general emotional and philosophical stance and its relevance to the matter at hand, than could be any summary by the narrator or analysis by another character (*CD*, V, 37–8).

The limitation of the narrative technique employed in *Call for the Dead* and *A Murder of Quality* is that it fails to provide the distancing required if the reader is to respond to Smiley as an ideal as well as a fallible human being. Not only does the unrelenting record offered of his inner life place too much emphasis on Smiley's qualms about, rather than considerable success in what he does but, by forcing him to carry so much of the narrative burden, le Carré somewhat trivializes his mental activities. When Smiley muses on the existential implications of loving Ann, he is revealed as intensively human but retains a degree of *gravitas* that makes it quite plausible that he should function simultaneously in an heroic role. However, to allow his consciousness to be the source of much of the novel's satirical analysis, as it is in *Call for the Dead* and, even more, in *A Murder of Quality,* is necessarily to rob him of this weightiness. This is not to say that Smiley should never be observed as he reflects, for example, on his detestation of the Sawley Arms: 'That muted light in the hall was typical: inefficient, antiquated and smug.' (*MQ,* XI, 235). Such sensitivity to the pretentiousness and falsity that characterizes much of what he sees around him is an essential part of Smiley's personality and similar thoughts pass through his mind at some point in every novel in which he appears. In *Smiley's People*, for example, he works with the narrator to anatomize the fake antiquity of the café in Thun: 'What else was there to look at? The lamps were wrought iron but the illumination came from a ring of strip lighting round the ceiling and it was very harsh' (XXIII, 266). What is needed, though, is a method of narration which provides le Carré with other media through which to express his broad satirical concerns and thereby leaves him free to cast Smiley in the role of satirist, only to the extent that it contributes to our understanding of the character.

Because he is so firmly wedded to third-person narrative throughout his first two novels, le Carré has to rely to a large extent on the sense of authority that Smiley acquires from his identification with the narrator to create an heroic dimension for his character. However, he does employ two other techniques which allow him to realize, at least partially, his intention that Smiley should function as an ideal. First, occasional switches are made in narrative focus to provide external and admiring views of Smiley. The effect of such changes in point of view is to produce a shift in Smiley's status from subject to object. Thus, a character the reader is accustomed to see as an earnest and often confused toiler, who can barely cope with the complex problems set for him by the tasks of daily living, is suddenly revealed to be a person of exceptional control and grace. Mendel is the source of one such change in perspective: 'He liked people who looked after things, who finished what they began. He liked thoroughness and precision. No skimping' (*CD*, X, 76), and Ailsa Brimley of another:

> Miss Brimley, watching him, wished she knew a little more about George Smiley, how much of that

151

diffidence was assumed, how vulnerable he was.

'The best,' Adrian had said. 'The strongest and the best'. (*MQ*, II, 168)

Second, Smiley's role is similar in a number of respects to that of the classic detective and he thereby acquires some of the aura that surrounds this genre fiction version of the archetypal hero. Like Sherlock Holmes, Hercule Poirot or Peter Wimsey, Smiley enters a usually placid and secure corner of English society – suburban Walliston in *Call for the Dead* and Carne School in *A Murder of Quality* – which has been thrown into disarray by an act of bloody murder. Temporarily all is confusion and even the most innocent become stained with suspicion of guilt. The victim in *Call for the Dead* is, for example, thought to have killed himself and the child-like and harmless Janie Lyn is arrested for the murder of Stella Rode. Eventually, however, the detective's almost superhuman powers of deduction reveal the identity of the guilty party and order is restored within the community. So as to place Smiley's activities firmly within this tradition of detection, le Carré allows him to provide, in both novels, a detailed account of how he untangled the complex knot of the crime. Thus, at one point in *Call for the Dead*, Smiley 'began, stage by stage, to recount as dispassionately as possible the sequence of events' (XIII, 103) and at the end of the novel he summarizes the problem which faced him and the steps he took to solve it (XVII, 133–41). In *A Murder of Quality*, he engages in a similar gathering together of clues (XI, 236–7) and brings the novel to its climax in authentic style by summoning the guilty party into the dining room and explaining in detail why he must be the murderer (XX, 282–7).[15]

[15] For a discussion of the formulas of the classic detective novel, see John Cawelti, *Adventure, Mystery and Romance* (Chicago, University of Chicago Press, 1976), pp. 80–97.

However, there are two problems associated with le Carré's extensive reliance on the conventions of the classic detective novel. First, the lengthy case summaries required by the genre are dull, appear contrived and seriously impede the narrative flow. Second, and more important, the entirely rational model of behaviour to which the classic detective conforms, does not allow sufficient scope for le Carré to express his conception of Smiley's character. Consequently, in *Call for the Dead* and *A Murder of Quality*, le Carré's claims that Smiley moves towards complete humanity by bringing the full resources of his personality – both reflective and emotional – to bear on the world around him, have to be constructed on an extremely artificial division of experience into separate categories, some to be dealt with by feeling and some by reason. Smiley's naive qualities are prominent at the beginning of his cases because they are the source of the deep concern for other people that gives him the energy to act on their behalf. It is also evident, as his investigations draw to a close, that the ability to feel has enabled Smiley to escape the kind of dehumanization that can result from the lies, deceit and role playing that his trade requires of him. Smiley may manipulate the objects of is investigation as he moves towards the solution of their crimes, but he never ceases to respond to them as human beings. As a result he is never in danger of becoming one of 'the living dead' (*MQ*, XX, 286), as he describes Fielding and Stella Rode, the other great actors in *A Murder of Quality*.

However, the emotions have no useful function to perform while Smiley is conducting his investigations. Indeed, that same concern for Mrs Fennan which helps keep him human, also blinds him to her lies and transforms him into 'the fool of his own sentiment' who has 'played false with the power of his mind' (*CD*, XIV, 112). The mysteries in which she entangles Smiley are not dissipated until he brings them entirely within the scope of his reason and approaches them as 'an academic exercise without reference to personalities' (*CD*, XIV, 112).

*Tinker, Tailor, Soldier, Spy,* the next novel in which Smiley plays a central role, is distinguished most obviously from *Call for the Dead* and *A Murder of Quality* by its much more flexible use of third-person narrative. As before, le Carré tends to filter each piece of action through the consciousness of a single character, but in *Tinker, Tailor, Soldier, Spy* that character is far less likely to be Smiley. This is partly because the plot of *Tinker, Tailor, Soldier, Spy* is triple rather than single-stranded and Smiley plays no part in Guillam's private life and has only a limited involvement in the activities of Roach and Prideaux. Events that centre on Thursgood's school are viewed first from Roach's perspective and later from Prideaux's, and Guillam tells his own story throughout. However, it is also because even those parts of the action which focus on Smiley are frequently presented from the point of view of another character.

The dispersal of the narrative burden amongst a number of characters deprives le Carré of the close identification between narrator and central character so important in establishing Smiley's sense of authority in *Call for the Dead* and *A Murder of Quality,* but, on the whole, it enables Smiley to fulfil his simultaneous functions as flawed human being and ideal much more effectively. As in his earlier novels, le Carré makes the direct presentation of Smiley's mental processes his major technique for communicating the character's intensely human concerns, complexities and confusions. However, because his is now only one of several centres of consciousness available to the author, le Carré is able to be much more selective about when he enters Smiley's mind. Thus, while Smiley's thoughts are, as before, the source of some of the novel's social satire, usually the reader is allowed to overhear only his most significant musings on topics such as Ann's infidelity or his conflict with Karla.

The sixteenth and seventeenth chapters, which are filtered entirely through Smiley's consciousness, are typical in their emphasis. For much of the time Smiley functions simply as an objective reporter who records what he reads and remembers as he works his way through files related to Control's conflict with Alleline. Only one satirical reflection interrupts the narrative flow, when he observes to himself of Alleline's motives for promoting Witchcraft: 'And there is the question of Alleline's greater glory' (*TT*, XVI, 134). However, a much more extensive diversion into Smiley's mental world occurs when a reference in the files to Bill Haydon sparks off an intense reflection on the state to which his relationship with Ann had been brought by her affair with Haydon: 'They shared no harmony. They had lost all calmness in one another's company; they were a mystery to each other, and the most banal conversation could take strange, uncontrollable directions' (XVII, 143).

The Smiley created by these very selective inner views is as fully human and fallible as the one presented in *Call for the Dead* and *A Murder of Quality*. However, the greater dignity he acquires from the increased emphasis on his loftiest concerns makes Smiley's human function more readily compatible with le Carré's efforts to provide him with a simultaneous heroic role. The success of these efforts in *Tinker, Tailor, Soldier, Spy* owes quite a lot to le Carré's reformulation of Smiley's relationship to the detective archetype, as we will see later, but even more to his flexible use of third-person narrative.

The presence in *Tinker, Tailor, Soldier, Spy* of a number of centres of consciousness allows le Carré to extend the technique used occasionally in *Call for the Dead* and *A Murder of Quality* of offering external admiring views of

Smiley which contrast sharply with the impression created from within. In part these views consist, as they did in the earlier novels, of simple eulogies: 'That one won't crack, though, Mendel decided with approval; one of your flabby oak trees, Smiley was. Think you could blow him over with one puff but when it comes to the storm he's the only one left standing at the end of it' (*TT*, XXXV, 316). However, le Carré's use of Guillam is rather more sophisticated than this. Guillam occasionally makes summarizing observations on Smiley's greatness, but more often he offers a running commentary on him as he employs techniques of interrogation and persuasion, the full implications of which are beyond his observer's grasp. When Smiley pursues his questioning of Ricki Tarr by warning him that his 'whole future stands by' (*TT*, XXII, 186) his answer to the question of what he did with the Swiss passports, Guillam reflects, 'and a lot more besides ... a whole chunk of devious arithmetic was hanging by a thread, if Guillam knew Smiley at all' (*TT*, XXII, 186–7). Similarly, during Smiley's later encounter with Toby Esterhase, Guillam notes that after a particular response, 'Smiley ... appeared momentarily set back', and infers from this 'that he was doubtless very pleased with himself' (*TT*, XXXIV, 304). The effect of scenes such as these is to transform Smiley into a rather mysterious and remote figure whose talents are of such a special kind that they defy rational analysis. Thus, Guillam's inability to do any more than offer appreciative but uncomprehending glimpses of Smiley comes to form a major part of le Carré's definition of him as a great man.

It is not, however, only through their direct comments that these alternative centres of consciousness help to add an heroic dimension to le Carré's presentation of George Smiley. Because so much of the action of *Tinker, Tailor, Soldier, Spy* is located in the consciousness of Prideaux,

Roach and Guillam, le Carré is able to establish quite firmly that, like Smiley, these characters are engaged in the pursuit of a better sense of self. Consequently, it becomes possible for le Carré to place Smiley for the first time within a finely graded moral spectrum. In *Call for the Dead* and *A Murder of Quality*, Smiley's obvious superiority to worthless bureaucrats such as Maston and 'chameleons' (*MQ*, XX, 286) such as Fielding and Stella Rode offers only the broadest affirmation of his goodness. However, demonstrations of his superiority to characters whose goals are as distinguished as his own, and who therefore function as rival heroes, does a good deal to confirm his greatness.

Le Carré's first description of Smiley in *Tinker, Tailor, Soldier, Spy* clearly establishes this comparative technique: 'Unlike Jim Prideaux, Mr George Smiley was not naturally equipped for hurrying in the rain, least of all at dead of night. Indeed, he might have been the final form for which Bill Roach was the prototype' (*TT*, II, 23). Prideaux's virtues are various; he is a courageous and loyal agent and a warm and caring human being. But Smiley has also proven himself in the field and his concern for Control, Ann and Prideaux runs as deep as Prideaux's for Haydon and Roach. In addition, Smiley has a sophisticated grasp on and ability to deal with the corrupt nature of reality that Prideaux completely lacks.

Roach is another exceptional character, in that he possesses an 'imaginative genius' (*TT*, I, 12) which gives him some profound insights into the reality that lies beneath the surface of things. He recognizes intuitively, for example, that Jim Prideaux's rakish exterior conceals intense pain. Smiley is, however, in possession of a very similar faculty which reveals itself most tellingly during *Tinker, Tailor, Soldier, Spy* in his early perception that Haydon is the traitor. In other respects, Smiley is very much Roach's superior. Both are, for example, outsiders and, indeed, their sensitive insights are in part a product of their isolation from the mainstream. In general, though, Roach finds his position oppressive and frequently allows it to victimize him; Smiley, on the other hand, as a comparison with Prideaux has already suggested, copes well with the world even though he is very much troubled by it.

There is also much to be admired in Peter Guillam, who is a loyal friend and a faithful servant of his country. Smiley, however, not only matches him in these areas but, as his ability repeatedly to baffle Guillam has already revealed, is very much his intellectual superior. Guillam's response to the world is, by comparison with Smiley's, primitive and crudely emotional. When Ricki Tarr behaves obnoxiously, Guillam explodes in useless anger. Smiley, on the other hand, remains calm and patiently guides Tarr back into the path he wants him to take. Guillam's loyalty to the Circus is also blind and unthinking, with the result that he is poorly equipped to deal with evidence of treachery in its ranks. Any allegiance Smiley owes to the Circus is, by contrast, based on a full knowledge of its darker side. Smiley's superiority is most evident, however, in that it takes Guillam until the end of *Tinker, Tailor, Soldier, Spy* to realize that his primary commitment must be to individuals rather than institutions and that love is the most important of all the emotions, and therefore for him to arrive at the starting point of what has been his colleague's life-long journey.

Besides providing scope for more external views of Smiley and for his placement within a moral hierarchy, the greater distance at which le Carré often operates from his central character's thought processes in *Tinker, Tailor, Soldier, Spy,* also allows him to make some revisions in his relationship to the classic detective hero. Le Carré has compared this novel to a country house mystery and clear links still exist between Smiley and the typical hero of works by Doyle, Christie or Sayers.[16] His mode of operation, for example, more closely resembles that of a detective than a secret agent in that, rather than plunge violently into enemy territory, he stays close to home and occupies himself with sifting evidence and interviewing suspects and sources. However, Smiley no longer conducts his enquiries in accordance with the narrowly rationalistic model offered by the detective novel. Instead he functions in a less precise but more complex fashion that calls into play all his mental resources, both naive and sentimental.

Le Carré is able to offer this revised version of his hero's investigative procedures not just because he is less wedded to the conventions of the detective novel but because he now has command of the techniques needed to create a convincing picture of the way in which such a mind works. The narrative method employed in *Call for the Dead* and *A Murder of Quality,* whereby much of the action is presented from Smiley's point of view, inevitably brings into great prominence the character's conscious, rational patterns of thought. In *Tinker, Tailor, Soldier, Spy,* on the other hand, le Carré operates at much less close quarters with Smiley and is under no compulsion to follow every twist and turn of his mind. He is thus free to create a rather impressionistic picture of how Smiley thinks, which can offer hints about the part played by intuition and instinct as well as recording something of his logical and meticulous sifting of evidence.

This new technique is well illustrated by the passage which describes how Smiley establishes, from documentary

[16] In an interview with Robert McNeil preceding the PBS showing of a televised version of *Tinker, Tailor, Soldier, Spy,* le Carré draws a parallel between this novel and the country house murder mystery. See also, Hopcraft, 'How Smiley Came to Life', p. 108.

evidence, the links between the mole Gerald and Source Merlin. Le Carré begins by providing some information about the nature of the files that Smiley consults and the kind of connections he is trying to establish between them. However, he does not go on to trace in any detail how Smiley achieves his goal. Part of his reason is that, as a maturing artist, le Carré has come to recognize how tedious and retarding of the action exhaustive analyses of the kind offered in his first two novels can be. But more important, he wants to avoid reducing the process in which Smiley is engaged to the merely rational. Therefore, rather than try to explain exactly what Smiley does, le Carré offers a metaphor intended to capture something of the rather mysterious combination of logic and intuition that moves him towards a solution of the puzzle he has set for himself:

> At this point, his mood could best be compared with that of a scientist who senses by instinct that he is on the brink of a discovery and is awaiting any minute the logical connection. Later, in conversation with Mendel, he called it 'shoving everything into a test tube and seeing if it exploded'. (*TT*, XXIII, 208)

The sense conveyed here, that the mind operates in ways that are beyond the control of even its possessor, is reinforced by le Carré's account of how what Smiley is looking for finally seems to emerge quite spontaneously from the files rather than as the inevitable end point of a series of logical moves on his part:

> And then he had it.
> No explosive revelation, no flash of light, no cry of 'Eureka', phone čalls to Guillam, Lacon, 'Smiley is world champion.' Merely that here before him, in the

records he had examined and the notes he had compiled, was the corroboration of a theory which Smiley and Guillam and Ricki Tarr had that day from their separate points of view seen demonstrated: that between the mole Gerald and the Source Merlin there was an interplay that could no longer be denied. (XXIII, 209)

Le Carré's redefinition of his hero's relationship to the detective archetype thus ensures that there is a much better match between the way in which Smiley conducts his investigations and the more general claims made about the vital role of both feeling and reason in his approach to experience. In addition, Smiley now emerges from a comparison with the detective type, that he still resembles in many respects, not merely as its equal but as its superior. Whereas Sherlock Holmes can solve anything accessible to rational analysis, Smiley is capable of penetrating the mysteries that lie at the very core of the human soul. Haydon's crucial lie concerning the source of his knowledge about Operation Testify (*TT*, XXVI, 228) is, for example, precisely the kind of clue that Holmes would have pounced on at least as quickly as Smiley does. For Smiley, however, such evidence is of minor importance in comparison to the understanding of Haydon's personality and motivations he acquires from his deeply intuitive apprehension of the significance of his affair with Ann.

In *Tinker, Tailor, Soldier, Spy*, then, le Carré finally succeeds in making Smiley perform two quite contradictory functions. Selective insights into his consciousness reveal him as a fallible and troubled human being, although one whose preoccupations tend to be of a rather elevated kind. The admiring views offered by other characters, comparisons with potential alternative heroes, and his transformation into a more complex and accomplished version of the detective archetype, afford him a truly heroic status.

So well do these techniques work for le Carré that, to a large extent, he uses similar methods to create the Smiley of his next novel, *The Honourable Schoolboy*. As in *Tinker, Tailor, Soldier, Spy,* so the narrative of *The Honourable Schoolboy* is filtered through several centres of consciousness besides Smiley's. Westerby's point of view, assisted briefly by Mama Stefano's, dominates a line of action that involves Smiley only at the beginning and the end. During other episodes from which he is absent, Craw, Connie and di Salis carry the narrative burden. When Smiley is the major actor he is, as before, frequently viewed from Guillam's perspective. The effect of such shifts in narrative focus is once again to create a balance between Smiley as he sees himself – a troubled, confused and anxious man – and the impenetrable, mysterious and apparently all-knowing person that others consider him to be. The emphasis placed on Westerby and his adventures also allows, as in *Tinker, Tailor, Soldier, Spy,* for Smiley's greatness to be defined through comparison with another, lesser seeker. Like Smiley, Westerby is concerned to reconcile the claims of the group with those of the individual. However, whereas Smiley proceeds by establishing a series of fine discriminations, Westerby is able to do no more than oscillate violently between unthinking loyalty to the Circus and total commitment to Lizzie Worthington.

Nevertheless, there are some significant differences between this novel and *Tinker, Tailor, Soldier, Spy* because in *The Honourable Schoolboy* le Carré is concerned to develop even further Smiley's role as an ideal, and he works hard at enhancing what Clive James, who does not approve at all, calls the novel's 'legend-building' tendency.[17] The most important innovation concerns the role

---

[17] 'Go Back to the Cold!', *New York Review of Books,* 27 Oct. 1977, p. 29.

played by the narrator. In le Carré's earlier works the narrator, although in part a centre of judgement, functions mainly as a neutral story-teller who stands firmly outside the action of the novel. This voice can still be heard in *The Honourable Schoolboy*, as, for example, in the crisp, detached account of Westerby's search for Tiny Ricardo:

> Jerry saw him just. The door of the little Beechcraft waited open for him, and there were two groundcrew poised to help him in. As he reached them, they held out their hands for the rifle but Ricardo waved them aside. He had turned and was looking for Jerry. For a second they saw each other. Jerry was falling and Ricardo was lifting the gun. (XVI, 379)

Frequently, though, le Carré adopts the very different persona of a man who reflects in a rambling and rather florid style on a world which he views from the inside. His knowledge, it seems, has come from case files, gossip and perhaps first-hand experience, and his narrative is both retrospective and tentative. The opening pages of the novel are dominated by this narrator as he reviews different theories of the origin of Operation Dolphin:

> Afterwards, in the dusty little corners where London's secret servants drink together, there was argument about where the Dolphin case history should really begin. One crowd, led by a blimpish fellow in charge of microphone transcription, went so far as to claim that the fitting date was sixty years ago when 'that arch-cad Bill Haydon' was born into the world under a treacherous star. (I, 15)

As le Carré's insider persona reconstructs the events of Operation Dolphin, so it becomes increasingly obvious that one thing above all remains impenetrable to him:

George Smiley's character. When Smiley withdraws to 'the inner regions of his solitary world' (IV, 94) in this novel, he leaves the narrator as far behind as he does Peter Guillam. Even as the action of *The Honourable Schoolboy* draws to a close the narrator is still fumbling for comprehension: 'And did Smiley *know* of the conspiracy, deep down? Was he aware of it, and did he secretly even welcome the solution?' (XXII, 531). The fog surrounding Smiley in *Tinker, Tailor, Soldier, Spy* has become thicker still in *The Honourable Schoolboy* and the reader, whose view is now often filtered through two pairs of admiring but uncomprehending eyes, is able to get few clear glimpses of him.

Le Carré exploits the increased distance at which he has set Smiley from the reader to begin the process of elevating his status from hero to legend. To this end, he frequently makes the narrator's function analagous to that of the hagiographer who, while unable to comprehend his subject fully, nevertheless collates reports of his greatness and struggles to discount heretical interpretations of his life. We thus learn from one source of Smiley's 'deft footwork' and 'technique' (I, 16) while a second comments, 'Poor old George: but what a mind under all that burden!' (I, 15). Yet another informs us that he is 'the last of the *true* greats' (I, 17). Any doubting voices are firmly suppressed by the narrator. Of those who criticize Smiley's handling of Sam Collins he says, 'They are talking simplistic nonsense' (X, 215), and he responds to claims that Smiley mishandled Westerby during the period of enforced idleness following the blackmailing of Frost, 'It is very hard to see what more he could have done' (XI, 239). The narrator is equally quick to squash the suggestion made by certain 'trivial critics' (XIII, 305) that Smiley should have recognized Westerby's growing infatuation with Lizzie Worthington: 'They might just as well have complained that he was a second-rate fortune-teller' (XIII, 305).

The idealizing tendencies inherent in the portrait of Smiley in *The Honourable Schoolboy* are further developed by means of yet another significant shift in his role as detective. In *Tinker, Tailor, Soldier, Spy,* Smiley's investigative methods are complex in that he proceeds by amassing pieces of information from a wide variety of sources, some of which serve as direct clues and some of which help him to achieve an understanding of the emotional context within which he is operating. The discovery of the existence of the safe house in Lock Gardens, for example, provides a vital clue as to how the mole Gerald communicates with the Russians. Details of Prideaux's mission into Czechoslovakia, on the other hand, are important mainly because of the insight they provide into the character and emotional state of Prideaux himself. The process by means of which Smiley synthesizes this diverse material is complicated and it calls into play, as suggested earlier, his total mental resources. However, le Carré simplifies Smiley's task quite significantly by remaining faithful to the convention of the detective novel which decrees that each piece of evidence shall be discrete. Thus, while Smiley's knowledge of Prideaux, for example, is derived from a number of sources – the files, Max, Mendel, Collins, Esterhase, and Prideaux – scarcely anything that he learns from one source overlaps with or is contradicted by another. Where this does happen – as in the differing reports of Control's competence during his final days – it eventually becomes clear that only one version of events is accurate. His task, then, can be compared to putting together a jigsaw puzzle that includes a few pieces from another box. Once the superfluous pieces have been cast out, all the others must, so long as sufficient effort and ingenuity are expended, fit together into a single, coherent picture.

In *The Honourable Schoolboy,* however, information tends to come to Smiley in a much more confusing fashion.

The various accounts he receives of Lizzie Worthington, for example, from Peter Worthington, her father and mother, Ricardo, Charlie Marshall, Sam Collins, and Westerby, do not lock together neatly nor does one entirely exclude any other. The essence of Lizzie's personality must, then, be extricated from a multi-faceted portrait of her as, in Westerby's words, 'suburban bolter. Ricardo's pupil and punchball. Charlie Marshall's big sister and earth mother and unattainable whore. Drake Ko's cagebird. My dinner companion for all of four hours. And to Sam Collins ... what had she been to him? ... A coat-trailer on probation ... the archetypal Woman Never to be Recruited' (XVIII, 450). For Smiley to succeed in making sense of the Lizzie Worthington puzzle, as he does by a process far too mysterious to be shared with the reader and so completely that he is able to make her the fulcrum around which the final stages of Operation Dolphin turn, transforms him into a detective of a very different order from any to be found within the classic tradition. His most obvious literary precursor is now Conrad's Marlow who strives throughout *Heart of Darkness* and *Lord Jim* to come to terms with the acutely contradictory but always in some way illuminating accounts he receives of the personalities and motives of Kurtz and Jim, the objects of his investigations.

Although *The Honourable Schoolboy* is even more ambitious in terms of technique than *Tinker, Tailor, Soldier, Spy*, it is possible that in directing much of his innovative impulse towards the problem of idealizing Smiley, le Carré has upset the delicate balance, so well established in the earlier work, between the two aspects of his major character's dual function. Nevertheless, the novel's achievement is considerable and seems almost to have exhausted le Carré's resources for giving expression to his vision of George Smiley. Thus, his next and final recreation of Smiley differs in only one important respect from those which have gone before. Instead of trying to maintain a balance between inner and outer views of Smiley, as is the case in the earlier novels, in *Smiley's People* le Carré deliberately fractures his presentation of the character into two halves.

In order to put the reader into close contact with the workings of Smiley's mind during the early parts of *Smiley's People,* le Carré reverts to the fairly strict version of third-person narrative employed previously in *Call for the Dead* and *A Murder of Quality,* in which most of the action is filtered through the consciousness of the central character. As a result the reader is given access to Smiley's thoughts on a wide variety of topics of varying degrees of weightiness. On his first appearance Smiley reveals an old man's concern with his sleeping habits (*SP,* II, 33) and, after the inspection of Vladimir's body, he reflects on the décor of safe houses, death as truth, Ann's egotism, the tendency of Scots to become spies, Lacon's marriage and present loneliness and Ann's theology-student lover. Interspersed between these thoughts is a series of cynical observations on the more pretentious of Lacon's comments (IV, 42–50).

This, then, is an intensely human and fallible Smiley and there are only two hints in the opening chapters of *Smiley's People* of the heroic aspect of his role. One is provided by le Carré's insistence on drawing attention, in rather portentous terms, to Smiley at the beginning of the first two chapters even though he plays no part in them. Thus the novel's first words are, 'two seemingly unconnected events heralded the summons of Mr George Smiley from his dubious retirement' (I, 7) and the second chapter begins, 'the second of the two events that brought George Smiley from his retirement occured a few weeks after the first' (II, 27). The other hint is contained within the brief external view offered by the Detective Chief Inspector as he considers Smiley's legendary features: 'Not *one* face at all actually, the Superintendent reflected. ... More your whole range of faces. ... An abbey ... That's what he was, an abbey ... made up of all sorts of conflicting ages and styles and convictions' (III, 39).

However, as Smiley is drawn into the pursuit of Karla, so le Carré makes increasing use of those techniques which allow emphasis to be placed on his heroic function. Smiley's consciousness ceases to carry the entire narrative burden with the result that le Carré is free to enter his mind only at those times when he is preoccupied with issues of major importance, usually about Ann or Karla. Besides assuming responsibility for parts of the narrative, these alternative centres of consciousness also provide external views of Smiley. Typically, as in Esterhase's comment that Smiley has 'too many heads under his hat' (XX, 245), these are expressed in a tone of bemused wonderment. Occasionally even the narrator, although he is never as fully a part of the world he describes as he is in *The Honourable Schoolboy,* joins this circle of puzzled admirers: 'Again there is mystery about Smiley's decision not to reply to this question. Perhaps only his wilful inaccessibility can explain it; or perhaps we are staring at the stubborn refusal of the born caseman to reveal anything to his controller that is not essential to their collaboration' (XIX, 239). As the action draws towards its climax, so an entire scene, Smiley's crucial interrogation of Grigoriev, is presented by another consciousness which directs us to admire, if not entirely understand, the functioning of a great secret agent:

Once again, Toby insists on bearing witness here to Smiley's unique mastery of the occasion. It was the strongest proof yet of Smiley's tradecraft, says Toby – as well as his command of Grigoriev altogether – that

throughout Grigoriev's protracted narrative, he never
once ... departed from the faceless role he had
assumed for the interrogation. (XXV, 294)

Le Carré does not attempt to synthesize these two ways
of viewing Smiley until the last few pages of the novel. As
Smiley waits by the Berlin Wall for Karla to defect, he once
again becomes the narrative centre, and the reader has
direct access to his every thought as he reflects on the
methods he has used to achieve victory: 'On Karla has
descended the curse of Smiley's compassion; on Smiley the
curse of Karla's fanaticism. I have destroyed him with the
weapons I abhorred, and they are his. We have crossed
each other's frontiers, we are the no-men of this no-man's-
land' (XXVII, 324). However, the picture of Smiley's
fragile humanity thus created, is balanced by his almost
peripheral observation of what is going on around him
since he is placed at the centre of a group of admirers for
whom he is a great man about to achieve his greatest
triumph:

From the darkness around them, Smiley heard whispered voices and the swift, damped sounds of hasty
movement under tension. 'George,' someone whispered. 'George.' From a yellow phone box, an unknown figure lifted a hand in discreet salute, and he
heard the word 'triumph' smuggled to him on the wet
freezing air. ... Smiley heard something about 'claim-
ing the prize'. (XXVII, 325)

This view of Smiley is reinforced in the final paragraphs of
Smiley's People when the narrator's consciousness completely supplants Smiley's in order to offer a last look at
him as he performs the most legendary of all his gestures:
'From long habit, Smiley had taken off his spectacles and

was absently polishing them on the fat end of his tie, even though he had to delve for it among the folds of his tweed coat' (XXVII, 327).

It would seem that le Carré structures the narrative of *Smiley's People* in the way described because he wants to establish a firm connection between Smiley's legendary status and his involvement in and mastery of the arts of espionage. Thus, while the presentation of Smiley in retirement and during his initial cautious probings around the edge of the case is a deeply sympathetic one, it is of an essentially ordinary man. Not until Smiley begins to function completely as a spy does le Carré construct his narrative in ways that reveal him to be a character of heroic proportions. The problem with le Carré's decision to manipulate his presentation of Smiley in order to emphasize a single, if important, point is that it sacrifices the kind of continuous complexity that makes our encounters with the character so satisfying in *Tinker, Tailor, Soldier, Spy* and *The Honourable Schoolboy*. The synthesis offered at the end of *Smiley's People* does not begin to compensate for this lack.

In that George Smiley never changes in essentials during the course of a number of fictional appearances that span nearly twenty years, he is similar to the recurring heroes employed by other writers of detective and espionage fiction. Richard Hannay's career and personal life progress considerably in the course of John Buchan's *The Thirty-Nine Steps, Greenmantle, Mr Standfast* and *The Three Hostages*, but his personality and attitudes are much the same at the end of these novels as they are at the beginning. Similarly, although James Bond has a number of significant experiences, including the loss of his wife and brainwashing by the Russians, he is scarcely altered by them. In the case of writers such as Buchan and Fleming, lack of development is an inevitable consequence of the extremely

limited way in which they conceive of their central characters. Composed around a handful of gestures and a few
simplistic attitudes and ideas, Hannay and Bond lack the
well-defined and complex core of personality needed to
provide a basis for plausible shifts in outlook or role.
There are, however, rather more positive reasons for the
absence of change in George Smiley. From his first appearance Smiley possesses a well-developed and comprehensive
world view which commits him to the task of holding in
balance forces that are essentially irreconcilable. Consequently, unless he completely alters his approach to experience, Smiley can never progress because he can never reach
what he is striving towards. Rather than tracing development, then, Smiley's various fictional appearances record a
series of heroic but inevitably unsuccessful attempts to
weld the differing circumstances with which he is faced
into a harmonious whole.

That Smiley is indeed complex despite being unchanging
is indicated by le Carré's various attempts to express his
vision of the character. The same conception underlies
every version of Smiley, but each is made different by the
new methods which le Carré employs to create a balance
between inner and outer views of the character, and hence
to reveal him as at once a completely fallible and confused
human being and a towering ideal. A reading of all the
Smiley novels is a satisfying experience, then, not only
because it allows us to grasp properly the range of problems that the world sets him and his persistence in trying to
solve them, but because it enables us to trace the process
by which le Carré builds on the lessons of *Call for the
Dead* and *A Murder of Quality* to create in *Tinker, Tailor,
Soldier, Spy, The Honourable Schoolboy* and, to a lesser
extent, *Smiley's People* richly satisfying versions of his
central character.

# CHAPTER FIVE

# *The Little Drummer Girl*: A New Beginning?

L E CARRÉ'S NOVELS are the product of a unified and consistent imaginative impulse. If there is a single theme binding my discussions of philosophical concerns, symbolic landscape, the conventions of espionage fiction and the recurring role of George Smiley, this is it. However, in the earlier chapters I have done very little to find a place for *The Little Drummer Girl* within le Carré's canon. The omission has been deliberate, for there are sufficient questions about the relationship of this novel to those which precede it to merit separate discussion.

The most obvious has to do with the world it creates. *The Little Drummer Girl* is by no means the first of le Carré's novels to look beyond George Smiley and the Circus for its subject matter. *A Small Town in Germany* is located within the Bonn diplomatic ghetto and has as its agent-hero Alan Turner, a man unconnected with the Circus, and *The Naive and Sentimental Lover* abandons spying completely in order to explore the affairs of an emotionally frustrated pram manufacturer and a failed artist. However, it is the first non-Circus novel that le Carré has published for thirteen years and, more significantly, the first since he came fully to recognize the value of George Smiley as a focus for his fictional concerns. Consequently, the possibility that a decision to do without Smiley in *The Little Drummer Girl* heralds a shift in thematic emphasis needs to be considered much more seriously than was the case with similar decisions in the past.

The other major question is raised by le Carré himself, for it is evident from his comments that in his view *The Little Drummer Girl* is quite different from the novels which precede it. In an interview with Melvyn Bragg, for instance, le Carré explains that he now intends to keep his fiction as close as he can to contemporary reality because 'by the end of the Smiley books I'd gone too far into a private world'.[1] We have already had occasion to question the assessment of Smiley contained within this comment and there is equal reason to doubt le Carré's actual definition of what is new about *The Little Drummer Girl*. When le Carré speaks of dealing with 'contemporary reality' he seems to be announcing that his interests have shifted away from the relationship between the ideology of the group and the spiritual and emotional needs of the individual and towards political and even polemical issues. At least that is the impression conveyed by his apparent assumption that readers will react to the book primarily in terms of its position on the Israeli–Palestinian conflict: 'I'm pretty sure that I am going to attract a great deal of flak, particularly in the States, for even suggesting there is anything to put in the Palestinian balance.'[2] Obviously there is discussion within *The Little Drummer Girl* of the origins of the Middle Eastern conflict and of the objectives of the parties involved. However, this is relatively sparse and to look at the novel for an analysis of such issues is only marginally more useful than to read *The Honourable Schoolboy* for its views on the American involvement in Vietnam and Cambodia or *A Small Town in Germany* for

---

[1] 'A Talk with John le Carré', *New York Times Book Review*, 13 March 1983, p. 22.
[2] Paul Gray, 'In the Theatre of Deeds', *Time*, 14 March 1983, no page numbers.

173

what it has to say about Britain's role in Europe.[3] Never-theless, unhelpful as the author might be in interpreting the direction in which he is moving, his insistence that he is making a fresh start in *The Little Drummer Girl* still requires serious attention.

Countering such suggestions that *The Little Drummer Girl* is breaking new ground is some clear evidence of continuity between this novel and those which precede it. A number of casual and at times probably unconscious allusions to earlier works indicate, for instance, that le Carré had his total *oeuvre* very much in mind as he composed *The Little Drummer Girl*. Gadi Becker's de-scription of Rosalind in *As You Like It* as 'so many people under one hat' (III, 63) echoes Toby Esterhase's definitive analysis of George Smiley: 'George has got too many heads under his hat' (*SP*, XX, 245). Kurtz responds to un-welcome orders with a phrase previously used by Connie Sachs: 'Yes repeat no' (*LD*, VI, 117; *TT*, XII, 110). On another occasion he uses an expression, 'Roses all the way' (*LD*, IV, 74; *TT*, IX, 69), which is drawn from Ricki Tarr's colourful vocabulary. The Bonn of *The Little Drummer Girl* is permeated with that same 'throbbing, stately hum' (I, 4) of Rhine barges so often referred to in *A Small Town in Germany*. And Charlie and Rachel share their child-hood homes in 'Branksome near Bournemouth' (VI, 100) and Macclesfield (VII, 138) respectively with Stella Rode of *A Murder of Quality* (where it is spelt 'Branxome' (XIX, 273) and Mr Hibbert of *The Honourable Schoolboy* (XI, 243).

Elements of continuity are even more evident in the techniques employed in *The Little Drummer Girl*. While it

---

[3] As Julie Diamond puts it in her perceptive review of the novel, *The Little Drummer Girl* is 'about politics, but it is not political'. See 'Spies in the Promised Land', *Race and Class*, 25 (Spring 1984), pp. 35–40.

places much less emphasis on detection than does the Smiley series, its basic pursuit plot is common to all le Carré's spy fiction. As a novel of espionage *The Little Drummer Girl* has its closest affiliations with three novels: *A Small Town in Germany,* the main action of which also involves the discovery of the whereabouts of an already identified but hidden target; *The Looking-Glass War,* in which the training of the agent is also given considerable emphasis; and *The Spy Who Came in from the Cold* in which the success of the operation is equally dependent on the agent's ability to convince his enemies that he is loyal to their cause.

Description is employed only sparingly in *The Little Drummer Girl.* Nevertheless, when it is used, as in the sections of the novel set in Germany, it serves much the same symbolic ends as in le Carré's earlier works. For example, a Munich landscape which embraces the 'disintegrating' (II, 32) edifices built as part of the nation's attempt to give expression to the Olympic ideal and a 'high-gabled gingerbread house' (II, 34) in the centre of the city's mercantile district effectively embody the combination of spiritual poverty and material prosperity which lies at the root of the German psyche.

*The Little Drummer Girl* also has much in common with its predecessors in narrative method. The controlling point of view is that of an omniscient narrator. This narrator resembles most closely the complex persona adopted by le Carré in *The Honourable Schoolboy,* in that he functions at once as an objective reporter and a rather idiosyncratic commentator, who passes judgement on the world of the novel from a position within it. However, as is the case in each of le Carré's other novels, the narrator also frequently chooses to limit his potential omniscience by filtering the narrative through the consciousness of characters directly involved in the action. Charlie's point of view is favoured over any other, but her perspective is supplemented by several others, the most notable being Kurtz's but also Becker's, Alexis's, Litvak's and Ned Quilley's.

*The Little Drummer Girl* seems to tend simultaneously towards innovation and continuity and any attempt to find it an appropriate place within le Carré's canon must obviously be based on grasping the nature of the relationship that exists between these apparently divergent strains. This task can best be accomplished, I will argue, by analyzing the novel's new subject matter from the philosophical perspective employed by le Carré throughout all his earlier works. What such an analysis reveals is that his frame of reference remains essentially unchanged in *The Little Drummer Girl,* but its application to a social situation, the Israeli–Palestinian conflict, and a central character, Charlie, quite distinct from any dealt with previously, allows for a significant development and even enlargement in le Carré's world view.

## I

The opening pages of *The Little Drummer Girl,* during which the Bonn Embassy bombing and its investigation are described, focus almost exclusively on questions of national character and ideology, and a series of sharp contrasts are established between the West Germans, the Israelis and the Palestinians. The Germans, whose major function is to establish a connection with the world of le Carré's earlier novels, are presented as a neurotic, self-obsessed and torpid people whose vital human energies have been sacrificed to the creation of a 'massively prosperous capitalist economy' (I, 4); the Palestinians as savage murderers; and the Israelis as a morally earnest and energetic people able to respond with dignity and purpose to constant attacks on their fragile national identity.

Le Carré creates a powerful first impression of West Germany by shaping his description of Bad Godesberg, Bonn's diplomatic ghetto (I, 3), in such a way that it embodies some of the society's essential qualities. The most notable characteristics of the area are wealth, quiet and fertility. None, however, has positive connotations. Wealth is associated with 'security grilles' and thus with loss of communication; quiet with secrecy ('secretive gardens') and sleep (the bombing occurs as diplomats are rising for the day), and therefore not only with loss of communication but also of energy; and fertility, through the comparison established between 'vegetation' and 'roads' that are built 'slightly faster than they make their maps', with the aimless and useless expansion characteristic of a capitalist economy. Bad Godesberg is obviously not a place which has any connection with meaningful human activity or which contains any promise of illumination, and it is finally and decisively summed up as 'a Grimm's fairy-tale blackout'.

Le Carré adds a further dimension to his portrayal of German society by describing how the national press shapes its reports of the bomb incident in order to cater to the needs of a people unwilling to deal with hard facts or painful truths. The horror of the incident is thus made palatable by a sentimental transformation of the boy killed by the bomb into 'the Angel Gabriel' (I, 6), a martyr for both Christians and Jews. 'Concerned Germans' (I, 6) respond to the easy emotional *frisson* thereby provided with gifts of money, the only thing upon which they place any value, unneeded though it is in the actual situation. The press also ensures that the death of a Jew on German soil stirs up as few unpleasant feelings as possible in a people who have still not come to terms with 'their

unconquered past' (I, 7), by taking a simplistic and uncriti-
cally pro-Israeli line in all discussions of the Middle
Eastern conflict which lie behind the bombing.

This brief analysis of German society is completed by an
account of how its intelligence officers conduct their
investigation. Neither Dr Alexis nor his 'Silesian policeman' (I, 7) colleague, who represent the twin liberal and
neo-fascist strains present in contemporary Germany, has
the sense of purpose or moral commitment needed to
complete the task facing them. At root, both are concerned
only with their own careers and they devote far more
energy to eyeing each other's performance than to working
towards the capture of a brutal murderer. The incompetence and carelessness which result from such self-interest
are particularly evident in the Silesian's behaviour during
the final conference. So far as he is concerned, the opportunities for the pooling of information are of little importance. Instead, his goal is to capitalize on the personal
triumph of being chosen to run the meeting in preference
to Alexis and he directs all his efforts into putting on a
show that will impress the audience. As a result he
responds to questions asked by Kurtz while he is 'in the full
flight of his performance' (I, 21) as unwelcome interrup-
tions and fails to notice that he is being pointed towards
the identity of the bomber.

The Palestinians' first appearance is fleeting. Nevertheless it is marked by a level of energy which offers a sharp
contrast to the lethargy of the Germans. The contrast does
not, however, work to the Palestinians' advantage for it is
created by changing the gently soporific landscape of Bad
Godesberg into a place of chaos and carnage:

All they could speak of, if they could speak at all, was
the road tipping, or a chimney-stack silently lifting off
the roof across the way, or the gale ripping through

178

their houses, how it stretched their skin, thumped them, knocked them down, blew the flowers out of the vases and the vases against the wall. (I, 5)

Vitality of the type provided by a bomb which leaves five dead and a child wounded clearly constitutes an even greater offence against the life principle than does the insidious process of atrophy produced by the Germans' lack of moral or spiritual force. The impression of the Palestinians as monstrous enemies of humanity is reinforced by the account of how they exploited the Israeli Labour Attaché's good will and spontaneous warmth in order to introduce their deadly package into his house: 'yes, he knew that suitcases could bite. But this was Elke's nice friend Katrin, from her home town in Sweden, who had received the suitcase from her mother that very day!' (I, 10).

Affirmative enough in itself, the portrait of the Israelis created during their initial appearance in the novel becomes all the more impressive when judged in relation to these negative appraisals of the Germans and the Palestinians. Like the Palestinians the Israelis have abundant energy but theirs seems directed towards creative rather than destructive ends. Thus, while Alexis and the Silesian continue to flounder, the altogether more dynamic Kurtz is soon able to give shape to the evidence collected about the bombing. The Israelis' success is not only the result of their leader's 'frantic and remorseless urgency' (I, 16) but also of a keen sense of shared moral purpose. For them, the bombing is the work of people dedicated to the destruction of Israel, and they are convinced that their efforts to eliminate the danger are conducted under the banner of justice. Because of this sense of purpose the Israelis are willing to probe more deeply – as in Kurtz's interview with Elke – and to deal with more awkward truths, such as the fact of the bereaved Labour attaché's adultery, than mere personal ambition can ever persuade the Germans is necessary. Something of the qualitative difference between the aimless, trivial Germans and the purposeful, morally earnest Israelis, is captured by le Carré's description of the postures adopted by each group as they wait for the closing conference to begin: 'The German contingent chattered and craned their necks at everything, including the Israelis, who for their part preserved the moral stillness of men for whom every wasted minute was martyrdom' (I, 17).

A clear sense is communicated here that the Israelis will serve as the first complete realization of le Carré's social ideals and this is reinforced by Charlie's subsequent comparison of Israel with Britain, a second country belonging to the sterile European landscape of the earlier novels. Britain, or at least the middle-class part of it, is characterized by Charlie as having entered a 'post-Christian era' (VI, 114) in which nothing has value except money and objects and the only sinner is the bankrupt. For her, Britain has experienced a *'castration'* of all traditions, faith and self-awareness and its joyless inhabitants are capable of no emotions other than 'apathy and fear' (VI, 114). Charlie's analysis is reinforced by Rachel who describes Macclesfield as death, 'the unhappiest place on earth' and condemns it for 'all that class and coldness and hypocrisy' (VII, 138). Israel, on the other hand, it appears to Charlie, possesses a reality entirely lacking in Britain, and its citizens with 'their action, their abstemiousness, their clear-eyed zeal, their authenticity, their true allegiance' seem able not only 'to fill the emptiness that had yawned and screamed inside her like a bored demon ever since she could remember' but also to give her a straight line 'after all her drifting' and a 'homeland at last' (VII, 138).

## II

As *The Little Drummer Girl* develops, however, the analysis offered in its first chapters, or at least that part of it which is concerned with Israel and Palestine, is revealed to be extremely misleading. Le Carré's cluster of national comparisons in fact constitutes not so much an introduction to the novel's argument, as a summary of the conventional western liberal view on the conflict in the Middle East. The actual task of the rest of *The Little Drummer Girl* is to provide a rather different and more discriminating perspective. The effect of this new perspective is to create a greater understanding of the Palestinian situation and to call into question much of what Israel does in the name of justice. It leads to the conclusion that the two countries are remarkably similar in their experience and in the ideological stances which they develop. Both win le Carré's admiration because of their vitality, commitment and sense of direction and because of their ability to forge deep and impassioned bonds between individual and group. In the end, though, he condemns each society equally for its cultivation of an ethic of hate which denies humanity to enemies and warps the humanity of its own members. By thus collapsing the moral distinctions established between the Israelis and the Palestinians at the beginning of the novel, le Carré not only challenges received opinion about the Middle Eastern situation, but also reveals the apparently new strain of social optimism implicit in his early comparison of Israel with Germany and Britain to be illusory. Far from providing an alternative to the sterile societies of his previous novels, the impassioned but destructive Israel fails just as

181

decisively to perform what is for le Carré the fundamental task of any social group: the development of institutions that will foster and give direction to the individual's instinctive imperative to love and care for others.

Clues to the direction which le Carré's analysis of Israel will eventually take can be found even within the generally affirmative opening section of *The Little Drummer Girl*. One is provided by a quickly suppressed newspaper article which suggests that the Israelis must take some responsibility for the Palestinians' barbaric action and another by Alexis's observation that Kurtz is 'possessed by a deep and awesome hatred' (I, 25). The fleshing out of these hints into a full analysis has two main elements. The first takes the form of a quite explicit if sketchy debate about Israeli ideology carried on throughout *The Little Drummer Girl*, mainly between Kurtz, Becker, speaking in his own voice and as the Palestinian Michel (whose real name is Salim) and Charlie, but with occasional contributions from others including the narrator, the Israeli Embassy's Press Officer, and Professor and Mrs Minkel. The second and more powerful is contained within le Carré's demonstration, by means of an exploration of Kurtz's actions and character, of the destructive effects on enemy and adherent alike, of the Israeli creed of hate.

The Israelis' view of the world is completely dominated by painful memories of past persecution of the Jews. Thus, in any situation of conflict they inevitably see themselves as innocent victims and look upon their opponents as the latest in a long line of oppressors bent on genocide. The Israeli Embassy's Press Officer firmly believes, for example, that unprovoked Palestinian aggression against a people who want to 'be left in peace' (I, 7) is the sole cause of the war between the two nations and that those responsible for murdering a single Jewish boy are inseparable from all previous persecutors of the Jews: 'Gabriel had died for one reason only: because he was a Jew. The Germans might possibly remember that Gabriel was not alone in this. If they had forgotten the Holocaust, perhaps they recalled the Munich Olympics of ten years ago?' (I, 7–8). For Kurtz, too, the Bad Godesberg bombing is yet another episode in the history of Jewish persecution and he calls on his agents to keep past attacks on their people in mind as they set out in search of Gabriel's murderers:

> A stone tablet, engraved in Hebrew and in German, commemorated the eleven dead in the Munich Olympic killings. Eleven, or eleven thousand, their feeling of shared outrage was the same.
> 'So remember that,' Kurtz ordered. (II, 33–4)

Given that the Israelis interpret all present situations in historical terms, it is axiomatic not only that their enemies must always be in the wrong but that, by setting themselves against the Jewish homeland, they have inherited the entire burden of guilt for the persecution of the Jews. As a result the Israelis respond to any situation of conflict with an enormous sense of moral righteousness. So far as Kurtz is concerned, for example, those who fight in the Israeli cause are primarily 'good and decent people' (VI, 103) and when questioned about what he wants to achieve from the war with Palestine, he is able to answer with the single, unequivocal word, 'Justice' (I, 24; XI, 202). As conflicts intensify so the conviction of moral superiority deepens. Any action taken by the enemy is regarded as a further contribution to the history of anti-semitism and is thus condemned as unjustifiable aggression which compounds the guilt of its perpetrators. Conversely, whatever the Israelis might do is entirely justified by the need to defend a weak but precious homeland against an implacable and brutal foe. This kind of discrimination underlies the very different terms and tones in which Becker and Kurtz talk about Palestinian rocket bombardments and Israeli air raids. Palestinian raids are a source of great indignation to Becker, and he describes them as vicious attacks aimed at the extermination of innocent and helpless people: 'Ask them in the kibbutzim to tell you about the whining of the Katyusha rockets, forty at a time, while they hide their children in the shelters pretending it is all a game' (X, 191). Israeli bombings, on the other hand, are necessary gestures of self-preservation and Kurtz speaks of their consequences in quite matter-of-fact terms: 'There were two sisters, but one of them had died in certain reprisal bombings we had to carry out south of the Litani River' (I, 25).

Self-defence, however, does not provide the only basis upon which the Israelis are able to reconcile a posture of moral superiority with a willingness to match and even to outdo every Palestinian atrocity. As far as they are concerned, any offence against the Palestinians is exempted from normal moral judgement because, by assuming the legacy of Jewish oppression, they have removed themselves from the human community. Kurtz, for example, provides what is in his view a complete justification for the planned murders of Salim and Khalil when he explains to Charlie that 'those who break completely the human bond . . . deserve to die' (VI, 107).

The case against Israel is directed at several targets. Charlie takes particular exception to the historical underpinning of Israeli ideology. On one occasion, for instance, she challenges the notion that all enemies of Israel belong within a tradition of anti-semitism by arguing that the Palestinians have quite different and legitimate ambitions for engaging in war with the Israelis: 'The Palestinians . . . are gentle, decent farming people of great tradition, unfairly driven from [their] land, from 1948 onwards, in order to appease Zionism – and make way for a Western foothold in Arabia' (X, 179). On another occasion she develops one of the major implications of this argument by suggesting that there is a good deal of hypocrisy in the Israelis' claims that they act only in self-defence: 'But only in self-defence. Israelis only ever kill in self-defence. ... You *are* bastards, aren't you? ... Because *you* get it both ways. One minute our bleeding heart, the next our red-toothed warrior. Whereas all you really are ... is a bloodthirsty, landgrabbing little Jew' (XIV, 242–3). In both of these instances Charlie is objecting to the Israeli tendency to use past experience to obscure present reality. It is therefore a logical extension of her argument that she should attack the special moral status demanded by and often accorded to contemporary Israelis because of the suffering of their Jewish ancestors: 'The Israelis can hack the Palestinians to pieces any time. But a couple of rabbis knocked off in Frankfurt or whatever – I mean that's a real grade-one prime-beef international disaster, isn't it?' (X, 191).

The Israelis' view of themselves as innocent victims, challenged in part by Charlie's explanation of Palestinian motives, is undercut from a different direction when Becker, speaking as Michel, points to their enormous military resources: 'To tiny, gallant Israel. ... To her amazing survival, thanks to an American subsidy of seven million dollars a day, and the entire might of the Pentagon dancing to her tune' (X, 185). His argument is reinforced by the narrator's account of the capabilities of the Israeli airforce: 'Israeli jets bombed the crowded Palestinian quarter of Beirut, in what was afterwards declared to be an effort to destroy the leadership, though there were no leaders among the several hundred dead' (III, 48).

However, the most serious of all the criticisms of Israeli ideology is contained within the rider which the narrator appends to his account of the Beirut bombing: 'unless of course they were the leaders of tomorrow, for many were children' (III, 48). Despite the almost offhand manner in which they are expressed, these are angry words, and they serve to communicate the narrator's total scorn for the notion that, by becoming the enemies of Israel, the Palestinians have sacrificed all claims to normal human consideration. His criticism is echoed by Mrs Minkel when she protests at the inhumane treatment of Palestinians in the occupied territories: 'In the Golan, the beatings and torture? On the West Bank, how they treat them, worse than the SS? In the Lebanon, in Gaza? Here in Jerusalem, even, slapping the Arab kids around because they are Arabs!' (XXIII, 372).

Although this debate is conducted only spasmodically throughout *The Little Drummer Girl* and the voices speaking out against Israeli ideology vary in quality, reliability and conviction, it has the overall effect of seriously undermining the position of authority granted to Israel in the novel's opening section. Now it seems that the vitality and sense of purpose so prominent there are founded at least in part on self-deceit, injustice, inhumanity and even paranoia. That this is the drift of the novel's ideological debate is confirmed suddenly and dramatically when Gadi Becker, who has previously spoken with vigour against Charlie's criticisms of Israel and who has shown a strong distaste for the views which he has been required to express in his role as Michel, reveals that he has been convinced by the case against his country. His change of heart manifests itself in the 'most offensive question' which he puts to an Israeli Embassy official: 'What are we to become, I wonder? . . . A Jewish homeland or an ugly little Spartan state?' (XXVII, 426).

However, powerful as its conclusion is, the main weight of le Carré's revisionist analysis of Israeli society is borne, not by this ideological debate but by his exploration of the consequences for the individual of complete acceptance of a social creed in which hatred and denial of humanity play such a major part. His case study is the Israeli intelligence officer, Kurtz.

Kurtz's own life is to a quite remarkable degree a reflection of the recent history of his race. As a child he suffers under Nazi oppression: 'Kurtz and his mother, and the hundred and eighteen other Jews who were crammed into their truck, ate the snow and froze, most of them to death' (II, 38). After the war he is among the first to settle in Israel and, during the period of the Mandate, is tortured by the British: 'They had imprisoned him twice and interrogated him four times, and the occasional troubles he had with his teeth were still ascribed by his dentist to the beatings he had received' (XVIII, 302). This education in suffering and victimization explains why Kurtz is so readily able to accommodate personal vision to national goals. For him, a 'frozen little boy' in a hostile world, Israel, a country shaped around a deep consciousness of the persecution of the Jews, is nothing less than a warm homeland that 'smelled of flowers' (II, 38).

The almost complete identification which he achieves with his society enables Kurtz to develop some remarkable powers, as we have already glimpsed in the earlier analysis of the first section of The Little Drummer Girl. Total commitment to Israeli ideology provides him with a sure sense of purpose, and this in turn is the source of an enormous vitality. Unlike Alexis, from whose perspective he is viewed at first, Kurtz is free of all burdens of self-doubt, egotism, or moral uncertainty and he seems capable of achieving any goal he sets for himself. For Alexis, Kurtz is nothing less than a hero, 'a giver of hope, a power-drill, a taskmaster extraordinary' (I, 14), an 'impressario . . . [a] manager . . . [a] general' (I, 15). This view is shared by

Kurtz's fellow Israelis: 'Kurtz cut the impossible path, Kurtz made the desert bloom. Kurtz . . . forced more good luck than the Jews had had for two thousand years' (II, 27).

But as *The Little Drummer Girl* develops, so it becomes increasingly obvious that Kurtz must pay a considerable price for his wholehearted commitment to a society whose ideology is dominated to such an extent by fear of annihilation and a sense of self-righteousness that it is unable to recognize the humanity of its antagonists. Much of what Kurtz does to further Israeli interests falls well within the normal range of espionage practice and is not very different, for instance, from what George Smiley does in the service of Britain. However, when Smiley lies, cheats, deceives and even kills, he is acutely conscious that, worthy as his goals might be, he is nevertheless offending against the humanity of a fellow being and is thereby compromising his own humanity. Consequently, the closer he draws to the completion of his mission the deeper becomes his anxiety about the moral and human implications of his actions. Smiley's thoughts as he waits in the Lock Gardens safe house for the arrival of the mole Gerald are typical: 'He had no sense of conquest that he knew of. His thoughts, as often when he was afraid, concerned people. He had no theories or judgements in particular. He simply wondered how everyone would be affected; and he felt responsible' (*TT*, XXXVI, 322). Because of this willingness to face up squarely to the significance of his actions, Smiley frequently manages paradoxically to affirm his humanity most completely at those very moments when he is placing it in the greatest jeopardy.

Kurtz, on the other hand, when put in similar situations, engages in very little self-examination because for him nothing can weigh in the balance against the Israeli cause and because he does not consider the enemies of his nation to be truly human. The way in which he responds to his Palestinian prisoner, Salim, is typical. Not only does Kurtz have no qualms about subjecting Salim to a programme of drugs and brainwashing but, as the mockery to which he subjects him even after he has been reduced to a 'collapsed puppet' (XIV, 237) reveals, he actually takes pleasure in the discomfiture of his foe: 'Now he's a great intellectual. Lot of money, lot of girls, good food, an easy time. That right, little fellow?' (XIV, 239). Perhaps because it also involves the killing of a young Dutch girl, the decision to execute Salim by bomb comes close to evoking a human response in Kurtz. However, any questions it raises in his mind are laid to rest once he has made the gesture of 'phoning his wife, thus reconfirming his ties to Israel. As Becker comments, 'Kurtz wanted to touch base before the killing. He wanted to hear Israel talking to him live' (XV, 251).

By exempting certain people from his area of concern in this way Kurtz inevitably diminishes his own humanity. The most obvious symptom of this is his increasing inability to acknowledge the unique existence even of those who are not the enemies of Israel. His admirer and ally, Alexis, is, for example, to Kurtz, despite considerable displays of friendship, simply someone to be used, and he speaks of him in the same dehumanized terms in which he refers to Salim and Khalil. Whereas Salim is 'Yanuka', the 'half-grown suckling' kid (II, 29), tethered to attract the lion Khalil, Alexis is 'a fine catch' (II, 28) or a sheep (XI, 204). When Alexis dares to break free from his assigned role by questioning the morality of the brutal murder of Salim, Kurtz no longer even pretends to treat him as a fellow human being, and resorts to bullying and blackmail in order to bring him back into line (XXII, 351).

Charlie too is less than human so far as Kurtz is concerned. He is effusively warm to her when they first meet. However, this is simply a piece of play-acting aimed at winning her commitment to the Israeli cause and on this same occasion Kurtz repeatedly reveals that he is interested in Charlie only in so far as she can be of use to him. What he wants is an actress. Therefore, he is pleased to discover that she is a liar because 'tomorrow she lies for us' (VI, 117) and, as she tells her life story, he pays far more attention to her technique than to what she says. Even after Charlie has proven her loyalty to the Israeli cause and has taken considerable risks to advance his mission, Kurtz cannot see her as anything other than a convenient tool. For example, he attaches no importance to the possibility that she might have been thrown into turmoil by her simultaneous involvement with the Israelis and the Palestinians because, 'what does it matter who she belongs to, so long as she keeps showing us the way?' (XXIV, 383).

The most striking evidence of Kurtz's dehumanization, however, is provided by his failure to grant independent human status to his long-time colleague and fellow Israeli patriot, Becker. For Becker, loyalty to Israel has become a very problematical business, and he experiences grave uncertainties about the direction which he should take in his personal and professional life. Kurtz can respond to his friend's dilemmas only by denying their legitimacy. Therefore, rather than try to understand why he has separated from his wife, Frankie, Kurtz repeatedly presses Becker to reestablish a relationship which conforms to the model of bourgeois Israeli respectability which he favours. On one occasion he even follows up a lecture on the iniquity of divorce by giving Becker's 'phone number to Frankie (XXVII, 427). Kurtz is equally dismissive of Becker's objections to resuming his career as an agent runner which he has given up as part of an attempt to remake his life: '*Do* it? He's an Israeli officer, Shimon. . . . First, I admit, Gadi said he would prefer to continue to study his new trade' (II, 41). However, the most extreme offence against Becker's humanity occurs when, rather than allow him to explore the disgust he clearly experiences at the brutal killing of Salim and his girlfriend, Kurtz simply bullies him back into conformity: 'You wish to tell me something, Mr Becker? You have a moral point to make that will ease you into a nice frame of mind?' (XV, 253).

Contained within le Carré's presentation of Kurtz, then, is a damning indictment of Israeli ideology. Complete acceptance of his society's values gives Kurtz remarkable purpose and energy, but the channelling of this energy into hatred of the enemies of Israel has begun a process at the end of which he is unable to respond to even his closest friends. Kurtz is, finally, as is suggested at various points in the novel, a tyrant (VII, 142), a man completely lacking in 'moderation' (XXII, 351), and a 'fanatic' (XVIII, 301), and the country which has produced him is, despite its ability to win the complete loyalty of its citizens, as far from fulfilling its obligations to nurture their humanity as any of the sterile communities presented in this and in le Carré's earlier novels.

Le Carré further develops his critique of the ideology of hatred by means of his presentation of the Palestinian perspective on the Middle Eastern conflict. Seen through their own eyes the Palestinians are not at all the mindless thugs they appear to be in the first chapter of *The Little Drummer Girl*. Acts of aggression such as the bombing of the Israeli Labour Attaché's house are, they would argue, the legitimate response of a victimized and almost helpless people to a more powerful enemy who, not content with robbing them of their land, is now bent on their complete destruction. The Palestinian case is made out in part, as we have already seen, by Charlie, Becker speaking as Michel, and the narrator, who combine to transfer to them the role

191

of morally righteous victims previously claimed by the Israelis, and in part by Khalil, who offers a rationale for his nation's campaign of terror. According to Khalil acts such as the proposed assassination of Professor Minkel, 'a nice person' (XXV, 398), are justified because they are a response to Israeli aggression and because they are directed against a people who have sacrificed all claims to humanity by murdering 'innocent' (XXV, 398) Palestinian women and children, and will therefore advance the cause of 'love and justice' against the forces of 'fear and ... hate' (XXV, 399).

Nowhere in *The Little Drummer Girl* is the Palestinian interpretation of recent Middle Eastern history seriously challenged. It would thus seem that for le Carré the Palestinians' characterization of themselves as 'the new Jews' (X, 181) is a more accurate reflection of contemporary reality than the Israelis' insistence that they are experiencing today the victimization which has always been the lot of the Jewish people. However, for all that the premise upon which it is founded may be correct in this instance, le Carré is no less critical of the creed of hate which the Palestinians construct out of their experience of oppression and consequent sense of moral superiority than he is in his exploration of Israeli ideology.

Part of this critique is contained within Charlie's damning analysis of the self-destructive spiral of reprisal and counter-reprisal into which the Palestinians have locked themselves with the Israelis as a result of their shared ideology of hate. The answer to the question of why the crippled Khalil continues to make his own bombs,

> was in everything she had seen since the night she had signed on with the theatre of the real. For Palestine, it ran. For Israel. For God. For my sacred destiny. To do back to the bastards what the bastards did to me.

To redress injustice. With injustice. Until all the just are blown to smithereens, and justice is finally free to pick herself out of the rubble and walk the unpopulated streets. (XXVI, 417)

However, the main burden of le Carré's analysis is borne by his characterization of the two brothers, Salim and Khalil. Their personal history, like Kurtz's, is almost completely a mirror of their country's. While still children, Salim and Khalil are driven from their native village, El Khalil, by the Israelis and, in later phases of the war, they lose their father, mother, a brother and a sister. Both also suffer personally at the hands of the Israelis and of Palestine's Arab enemies. On one occasion Jordanian troops force them to beat each other's feet and on another occasion Khalil is beaten almost to death by Syrian soldiers and loses a hand to an Israeli bomb. As a result they find it easy to commit their entire selves to a Palestinian ideology constructed around notions of victimization, moral superiority earned through suffering, and hatred of Israel.

This identification of self with society makes it possible for Salim and Khalil to develop qualities of purpose, energy and passion almost as impressive as those possessed by Kurtz. Even his Israeli enemies are forced to acknowledge the passion with which Salim speaks of Palestine and Charlie needs only the briefest glimpse of him to recognize 'the light of rebellion in his coal-dark eyes' (XIV, 238). Khalil creates an even more powerful first impression: 'Once more, he was beautiful. He was Michel full-grown, with Joseph's abstinence and grace and Tayeh's unbothered absolutism. ... He was broad-shouldered and sculptured, with the rarity of a precious object kept from sight' (XXV, 397).

But Salim and Khalil are also like Kurtz in that both are ultimately dehumanized by directing their passions and energy into hatred of an enemy that they consider to be less than human. Terrorist acts are too offensive to Charlie's sense of humanity ever to be contemplated (VII, 128; X, 187). Yet for Salim and Khalil they raise no questions of conscience. As Salim describes terrorism, it is either a '*jehad*' or 'holy war' (XII, 210), or 'theatre' (XII, 212). Thus he clearly thinks of his targets as infidels or actors rather than as complete human beings. The brothers' scorn for the humanity of their victims is even more evident in the animal metaphor by which Salim defines their purpose: 'I have told you that terror is theatre, and that sometimes the world has to be lifted by its ears before it will listen to justice' (XII, 212–13). Such failure to recognize others as being human inevitably diminishes the humanity of Salim and Khalil, and neither is able to respond appropriately even to those who have not sacrificed all right to consideration by participating in the oppression of Palestine. The most horrifying example of this is Salim's decision to sacrifice a girl who has attached herself to the Palestinian cause by sending her on board a plane with a bomb in her luggage (XIV, 240). However, more generally representative of the two brothers' stunted human response is their tendency to view women as 'comfort girl[s]' (XV, 248) whose only role is to provide sexual recreation in the intervals between operations. Even Charlie, who goes to him primarily as a soldier involved in a dangerous bombing mission, is expected also to satisfy Khalil's sexual needs: 'Tomorrow night you will be more affectionate perhaps. With Khalil there can be no rejections' (XXIV, 381).

### III

By the time it is completed le Carré's social analysis is no less pessimistic in *The Little Drummer Girl* than in any of the novels which precede it. The enormous expectations which the book arouses about Israel through comparisons with Germany and Britain are eventually disappointed. Similarly, the tantalizing glimpses it gives of what might be achieved when individual and group draw close together are soon submerged beneath damning appraisals of Kurtz, Salim and Khalil. Indeed, because of its tendency to undercut early affirmation, *The Little Drummer Girl* might be considered the most cynical and ironic of all le Carré's works. However, if we turn now to the other main thread which runs through the novel – its account of how characters fare if they refuse to yield themselves up to dehumanizing social influences – it becomes evident that the book has more to offer than simply an intensification of the darkness which already pervades le Carré's world view. Of all the characters in earlier novels only George Smiley has any degree of success in undertaking a search for selfhood that must be conducted outside the context of supportive social institutions. And the best that can be said for him is not so much that he ever fully reconciles the disparate elements out of which his personality is composed as that he refuses to yield up the attempt. In *The Little Drummer Girl*, on the other hand, le Carré introduces a new heroine, Charlie, who comes very close to completing her quest for self and emerges at the end of the novel as a richly mature human being capable of entering into and sustaining a satisfying love relationship.

First impressions of Charlie are not promising. Her intentions are certainly sound enough in that she is committed to shaping her personality and way of being around a core of loving instincts described variously as 'warmth' (VI, 106), 'incurable goodwill' (III, 49), 'caring for the world' (III, 48) and 'natural humanity' (VI, 105). However, since the society in which she lives, a Britain characterized by 'the malign sloth of authority, the caged despair of the losers' (XIV, 246), offers her no support and since she lacks the reflective qualities which enable Smiley to construct general moral principles out of flashes of instinct, Charlie seems to have little hope of progressing towards her goal. The best that she has previously been able to do is to become involved in a series of radical movements which, if they ever achieve their aims, will reshape social institutions so as to make them compatible with her emotional impulses. Such involvements, however, amount to little more than quixotic gestures and it seems likely that in the future Charlie will remain hopelessly adrift unless she yields to the unequal struggle and seeks escape through total immersion in the illusory world of the theatre.

That things turn out quite differently for Charlie is entirely the consequence of her recruitment by the forces of Israeli intelligence for a new type of acting part in 'the theatre of the real' (XIV, 237) or 'the theatre of deeds' (VII, 139). As a path to salvation the theatre of the real is extremely dangerous because it is based on a number of deceptions, the most significant being that its *raison d'être* is the destruction of life and not, as Charlie believes, the cultivation of a relationship with 'a perfect lover whom she'd never met' (VII, 138). Nevertheless, close as it brings Charlie to disaster the theatre of the real proves to be a very useful deceit because it provides her, at least temporarily, with the sustaining context which she has always lacked in her efforts to create a complete *modus vivendi* out of her instinctual urge to love and to care for others.

Charlie is thus the first of le Carré's characters to be given the chance to play a part which gives shape to rather than denies instinctual urges. Those who act in earlier novels – and le Carré has always employed theatrical metaphors, particularly as a means of defining the spy's involvement in role-playing – do so to escape the self.

Included in this group are Elsa Fennan who hides behind a spying role which is quite literally played out in the theatre, since meetings with her control take place at the Weybridge repertory and Sheridan theatres, and Leo Harting, whose attempts to contort himself into shapes deemed appropriate by the diplomatic community are defined by dramatic imagery: 'He's a performer. He wears our clothes, uses our language'; 'He was ... an actor, I suppose' (ST, XIII, 219; XIV, 227). Even Smiley thinks of himself as going 'on stage' (SP, XXVII, 326) at those moments when his intelligence function demands that he behave in ways that contradict his instincts. Performance serves Charlie in much the same way in her career as a stage actress. Actors are, as Ned Quilley says, 'hollow vessels waiting to be filled' (IV, 79) and he describes Charlie as a 'chameleon' (IV, 76), a term previously associated with those consummate role players Terence Fielding and Stella Rode (MQ, XX, 286). However, acting imagery used in reference to Charlie's involvement in the theatre of the real – for example when she tiptoes 'gratefully to the wings' (VII, 136) to watch herself transform real anger into a performance of anger – has no such negative connotations because it defines a process in which the emotional and rational aspects of the personality function together rather than in opposition.

While playing her part in the theatre of the real Charlie is engaged in an emotional entanglement with the Israeli agent, Gadi Becker, and in a fictional ideal love affair with the Palestinian terrorist, Michel (VIII, 148–9). The interrelationship thereby established between feeling and the conventions of feeling is made even more complex by the fact that Charlie's love for Becker has its origins in and continues to be associated with a first meeting with him in the thinly fictionalized part of Joseph and by her eventual encounter with Salim, the real person upon whom the role of Michel is based. Charlie is therefore at last in a position analogous to that of the citizens in Schiller's ideal state, her script providing her with the guidance they received from social institutions, and by mediating between fiction and fact, idea and reality, in other words between the sentimental and the naive, it now becomes possible for her to know about feeling as well as to feel.

Charlie's success in acquiring this dual capacity is particularly evident in two situations. First, rather than allow her intense feelings to take complete control at the moment when she and Becker become lovers, Charlie maintains sufficient detachment to be able to make the experience richer by bringing to bear on it her earlier relationship with him in the role of 'the one incomparable lover she had never had' (XIX, 315). As she puts it: 'their whole shared fiction was nothing but foreplay for this night of fact' (XIX, 314). Second, faced with the suffering and pain of the Palestinian refugee camps, Charlie is able to summon up an emotional response sufficient to the enormity of the situation by drawing on the knowledge of feeling that she has acquired while playing Joseph's lover and Michel's grieving widow:

> And when the boys, over tea and cigarettes, regaled her with brave stories of their families' sufferings at the hands of the Zionists – just as Michel had done and with the same romantic relish – it was her love for Joseph once more, her memory of his soft voice and rare smile, that opened her heart to their tragedy. (XXI, 328)

Le Carré's portrait of Charlie is by no means entirely affirmative. She is able to come to terms with herself only because of the existence of special and quite transitory circumstances and once they cease to exist there is every possibility that she will lose all that she has gained. Realization that the actual goal of the theatre of the real is the murder of a Palestinian terrorist rather than the creation of a perfect love and that her final role is to be that of Khalil's whore rather than Becker's beloved – 'love was not their province: not his, not hers' (XXV, 409) – leaves Charlie 'without love and without value to herself' (XXV, 410) and 'dead' (XXV, 409). Thus deprived of an environment of love and too self-aware to gain satisfaction from the previously comforting illusions of the conventional theatre, Charlie finds herself caught in a situation at least as desperate as any that faces le Carré's earlier heroes.

However, having pointed his action firmly in the direction of failure, le Carré chooses to make Charlie's dark night of the soul a brief one. The circumstances that allow her quest to reach a positive conclusion serve to emphasize further the value of certain kinds of role-playing. At the beginning of his engagement in Kurtz's 'theatre', Gadi Becker, partly because it is demanded of him by his simultaneous function as agent-runner and partly because he has been drained of feeling by years of service in Israeli intelligence, is incapable of acknowledging his stirrings of affection for Charlie. However, the complete avoidance and retreat into self which this 'climber weary of the mountains' (XIII, 235) employs in other emotionally challenging situations, such as his marriage, are not possible on this occasion because he must persist in playing the role of Charlie's lover. Fiction is thus given the opportunity to create fact and as he acts out his part so Becker learns to feel again. The transformation which takes place is not at all smooth, and even after the significant moment when he makes love to her 'outside the script' (XIX, 313), Becker denies any personal commitment by pimping Charlie in the Israeli cause. In the end, though, he puts his feelings for Charlie ahead of any other loyalties and as a result, provides her once again with a loving and caring context. The novel's final scene is structured in such a way as to give full emphasis to the significance of their reunion. It begins on-stage where Charlie encounters love only in the meaning-less form that it assumes within the conventions of the romantic comedy in which she is playing. In the middle of her performance, however, she catches sight of Becker seated in the audience and immediately 'there was really no point in acting any more' because 'Joseph had become so real at last' (XXVII, 429). Thus, she steps down from the stage, passes through the lights that separate the playing area from the audience, and decisively exchanges the realm of illusion for a world of reality and love.

The union of Charlie and Becker with which *The Little Drummer Girl* ends is quite different from anything to be found in le Carré's earlier fiction in that it affirms the possibility not only that the individual can achieve complete and mature humanity but that the mature human being can find a role in the world. However, as is the case with the exploration of new social landscapes examined earlier, so elements of continuity are interwoven with those of change. Charlie's quest for self, and indeed that of Gadi Becker, are desperately difficult enterprises. The unique circumstances provided by the theatre of the real, some good luck, and perhaps the final triumph of the author's romantic spirit over his usual hard-headed real-ism, ensure that they are successful.[4] Nevertheless, during Charlie's encounter with Khalil and during her separation from Becker, it becomes clear that even an attempt to create a universe of two is probably more likely to fail than to succeed. The problem of how to be human in an

---

[4] For one critic at least the novel's ending is not so much romantic as 'maudlin' and 'kitsch'. See T. J. Binyon, 'Theatre of Terror', rev. of *The Little Drummer Girl* in *Times Literary Supplement,* 25 March 1983, p. 289.

inhuman world is therefore scarcely less impenetrable in *The Little Drummer Girl* than it is in any of le Carré's earlier novels.

The shape of le Carré's fictional world is not, then, drastically altered by *The Little Drummer Girl*. His social landscape is broadened and enriched by the introduction of Israel and Palestine, passionate societies which contrast so sharply with the sterile communities to be found in earlier novels, but its dark contours are in no sense lightened. And while Charlie comes much nearer to achieving personal resolution than any previous le Carré hero, the special circumstances in which she is placed and the closeness of her approach to the precipice of disaster lessen the impact of the novel's emphatically romantic ending. The story of this new heroine has a good deal to say about the positive function of role-playing in the individual's struggle to bring into harmony the warring elements of personality. However, as with the glimpses he allows his readers to catch of the ways in which a close relationship to society can sustain the individual, le Carré is as far as ever from allowing that such experiences might be possible for the great majority of us.

It is, of course, dangerous to offer conclusions about a writer who is in mid-career and who shows every sign of producing further novels. Nevertheless, the ease with which *The Little Drummer Girl,* a work which differs in so many respects from its predecessors and which breaks so sharply away from the *Quest for Karla* trilogy, can be accommodated within a canon that includes nine novels written over a period of more than twenty years, clearly suggests that le Carré's vision of the world is not an evolving one and that his concern in the future is likely to be, as it has been up to now, with the elaboration, development and modification of this vision rather than with the search for new perspectives. If such is indeed the case, then the present study of John le Carré's fiction, with its emphasis on recurring elements of theme and technique, should provide a basis for understanding not only the novels with which it deals but also those still unwritten.

# Index

203